Sample Excerpts From This Book

…We went to a Washington Senators day game. Ted Williams was the manager. They were awful. Naturally we had to have beer with us—we weren't going to pay the prices at the ball park. It's summertime, how are you going to sneak in beer? They caught us. Russert—who was eighteen—makes a deal with the guy at the turnstile, "How about if you just keep the beer here, and when we want one, we'll come back here and drink it in front of you?" The guy says "okay"—can you believe that? Only Russert would have the gall to even think of asking that.…

…When it rained at Woodstock, there was no cover. We decided that night that when we went back to the car that we would jump into the swimming pool. There were no lights there but we'd seen the pool when we'd walked by the farmhouse so we jumped in. Well, the next morning, the pool was filthy. It looked like an oil slick. Russert told Brokaw that it was used as a bathroom. It wasn't so much that, it was the people who'd gotten so filthy dirty in the rain on that muddy hillside. So unbeknownst to us, we weren't the only ones who used it…and we may not have been the first.…

…Notre Dame called and said, "We're sorry. Mr. Russert is running late, and won't be able to come." We were heartsick. I started to send people home. About ten minutes later my phone rang. It was Tim. He said, "Chief, I know what it's like to lose an interview. We'll be there. Don't send anybody home. I'm coming."…We were in my office. I had a White Board—just like his. Tim was staring at it. My daughters had been in my office the night before. They had written doodles on it: "You rock, Mom." "Love you, Mom." He looked at it and said, "You know, Chief, that's what life is all about. You should be so proud that your daughters would say that to you." It made my year when he said that. What a thoughtful man!…

Sample Excerpts From This Book

...Pat Hoak was diabetic. We were the only students on campus who were allowed a refrigerator so Pat could to keep his insulin refrigerated. Tim would always stop by our room 'cause he lived off campus. Tim would say, "Hoakie, you got to get rid of some of this insulin 'cause you're taking up all our beer room."

...We always used to make fun of Russert saying, "You can sell your bill of goods to all these people, but we know you from high school...!" He'd say, "Hey, keep this to yourself." ...Shirley was on the cafeteria front door, and you didn't get by Shirley without a meal ticket. Russert schmoozed Shirley, "Beautiful. Shirley, you look wonderful." "Oh, Tim," and he'd be in the door. Or, he'd be coming in the back door 'cause he had the key to the place....

I would be told, "Tim's gonna be in Chicago Saturday." I would have my list of Republican agenda things. I knew I had him. He couldn't possibly refute me. The last time I saw him, I was pent up about something and I was really ready to nail him. I see Russert coming toward me. "Hey Pacelli, what's going on?" Before I even said anything about "T.J. you ignorant slut," he would say, "Oh, J.P.'s at Yale now." He knew my son, J.P., had been a freshman at Tulane but had to transfer after Katrina. He had to reapply to schools. How did Tim know...he disarmed me! I forgot about my agenda.......Tim always had the classic line whenever I sent a friend to watch *Meet the Press* in person: "You tell Pacelli he still owes me fifty bucks!" Later on, it grew to a hundred....

Tim Russert,
We Heartily Knew Ye

Wonderful Stories from Friends
Celebrating a Great Life

RICH WOLFE

Published by Rich Wolfe and Lone Wolfe Press, a division of Richcraft. Distribution, marketing, publicity, interviews, and book signings handled by Wolfegang Marketing Systems Ltd.—But Not Very.

The author, Rich Wolfe, can be reached at 602-738-5889.

Cover design: Dick Fox
Interior design: The Printed Page, Phoenix AZ.
Author's Agent: T. Roy Gaul

International Standard Book Number: 978-0-9800978-4-9

Printed in the United States of America

10 9 8 7 6 5 4 3 2 1

DEDICATION

To Jimmy Crotty,
a fine Buffalo Irishman

ACKNOWLEDGMENTS

Wonderful people helped make this book a reality, starting with Ellen Brewer in Edmond, Oklahoma, and Lisa Liddy at The Printed Page in Phoenix, Arizona—wonder women who have been indispensable sidekicks for many years.

Special thanks to John Hrycko, Jim Young, Kristin LaGuardia, Patricia Higuera, Joe Liddy, Rob Lucas, Andrea Gonce, and Bobby Adams. Not to be forgotten are Deanna Bender of Middleburg Heights, Ohio and Barbara Jane Bookman, The Belle of Louisville, in Falmouth, Massachusetts.

And a big shoutout to Jann Wenner, Aimee Schecter, and Anne Marie at Wenner Publishing.

PREFACE

Just a few months ago, I was more likely to be struck by lightning while honeymooning with Christie Brinkley than to be writing a book on Tim Russert. You would have been more likely to see a left-handed female golfer than you were to read a book on the passing of Tim Russert. But, then, Tim Russert went marching home with a tint of a twinkle, a touch of class and a ton of intensity. Russert hung the moon and scattered the stars over NBC and America's political landscape. And now he's gone.

Growing up on a farm in Iowa, I avidly read all the Horatio Alger-style books of John R. Tunis, the Frank Merriwell collection and Clair Bee's Chip Hilton series, all which preach the values of hard work, perseverance, obedience and sportsmanship where sooner or later, one way or another, some forlorn, underweight underdog would succeed beyond his wildest dreams in the arena of life. Frank Merriwell, thy name is Tim Russert. Tim Russert was better than Frank Merriwell. He was real life...more natural than Roy Hobbs...a Rudy with talent. Russert was manna from heaven to the political spectrum and every other beleaguered TV talk show. Perhaps politics will survive the quagmire of idiots masquerading as politicians and TV hosts today...perhaps not.

> Tim Russert was better than Frank Merriwell. He was real life.

I only write books on people who seem admirable from a distance. The fear, once you start a project, is the subject will turn out to be a jerk. With Russert's intensity it could easily follow that he could be a self-absorbed, arrogant, rude boor, like most people in his business. As you will soon find out, you would want your son, your brother, your husband or your friends to possess these qualities of humbleness, thoughtfulness, joy for living, a passion for his job and the love of politics that Tim Russert had. If you are a certain age in this country, there are maybe three or four people in your lifetime that you remember where you were when you heard they had died—John F. Kennedy, Elvis, Princess Diana and, since you're reading this book, probably Tim Russert. On Friday, June 13, 2008, I was in Midtown Manhattan signing copies of my latest book, *For Yankee Fans Only, Volume II.*

Upon finishing the signing at the Yankee Clubhouse Store in Midtown, we were walking to the Port Authority to catch a bus to New Jersey. I glanced up at the scrolling news sign in Times Square. The sign said, "Tim Russert dies at age 58." I turned to my cohort and said, "Some company must be filming a movie here today." She asked, "Why do you say that?" "Look at that sign. It says that Tim Russert died. He couldn't have died. I just talked to him the other day." She said, "Well, it doesn't look like they are filming a movie around here. Maybe it's true."

"It can't be true." Just a few weeks before, on the way to a meeting at 30 Rock, we shared an elevator. I had never seen him in person before and was quite surprised at how big he was, particularly how tall he was. Knowing he was a big Yankee fan I flipped an extra copy of the new Yankee book to him and said, "Hey, Yankee fan, enjoy this on your next plane ride." The Yankee book is really different because, among other things, it has two dust jackets. The outer dust jacket comes off and opens up into a three-foot-by-two-foot poster, which is a combination of the *National Lampoon, Saturday Night Live, The Onion* and *MAD* magazine. Inside the book Yankee fans relate their neatest stories, topped off by sixty-four pages of color pictures. Each color page is a full-page reproduction of a cover of *Sports Illustrated* that the Yankees had once graced. A week or so later, my cell phone rang—my cell phone number is in the front and back of all my books—and the voice on the other end said, "Brother Wolfe, you wrote the neatest book in the history of the New York Yankees." The caller was Tim Russert. I couldn't believe that he took the time to make that call.

I had lost most interest in politics in recent years because some of us are old enough to remember when politicians were statesmen and not juvenile anarchists. The only political show I watch is *Meet the Press*, and only because Russert made it so interesting. The guy had magic on the air.

Even though I can't type, have never turned on a computer and have never seen the Internet, I've been very blessed to be able to do almost three dozen books using a format that is rather unique. Until now, all these books have involved sports. But a few years ago a famous conservative politician encouraged me to do a political book using the same format. After watching all the marvelous eulogies about Tim Russert, I decided, "Wow! Tim Russert could be my first non-sports book." A good decision in retrospect.

> ...Russert made it so interesting. The guy had magic on the air.

Of all the thirty-plus books, my favorite was a book on Tom Brady, the New England Patriots' quarterback. Upon completing the Russert book, it was apparent that there are incredible similarities between Tim Russert and Tom Brady...mainly their manners, their thoughtfulness, their kindness and—work-wise—how totally prepared, their work ethic and their incredible attention to detail. No wonder Tim Russert was so well liked.

Tom Brady is about twice as good a quarterback as most people think he is, and most people think he's great. Example: his coach, Bill Belichick has a record of 42-56 in the NFL without Brady as the starting quarterback. With Brady, Belichick's record is 101-27. Charlie Weis would never have been head coach at Notre Dame if it weren't for Tom Brady. The same thing could well be true of Russert. *Meet the Press* was going down the tubes until Russert took it over. We really won't realize how good he was until several years elapse and we have comparisons to make.... But sight unseen, the smart money is on Russert.

It's unusual to talk about Russert in the past tense because repeatedly, during interviews most of his friends and cohorts and colleagues would talk about him in the present tense.

After watching all the eulogies, most Russert fans knew what famous people thought about him. Over the years, I've often found that the very best stories come from the non-famous people who knew the subject when the person was younger and in less public surroundings. The same holds true for this book.

Particularly enjoyable were Tim's classmates at John Carroll University in Cleveland from which he graduated in 1972. Many college counselors often write that the best-sized school to attend would be any school under 2,500 because it seems like people from schools of that size develop more and longer-lasting friendships than they do at the larger schools. This certainly is true about John Carroll, and even more true, perhaps, about Tim's graduating class of 1972. What a great group of guys were at John Carroll at that time.

One of Tim's John Carroll buddies mentioned that Tim's eulogies and services were similar as if a congressman or a senator who died. On the other hand, Jesse Helms died at almost the same time, and he was a blip on the radar compared to the stories and adulation given Russert.

> ...about Tim's graduating class of 1972. What a great group of guys were at John Carroll...

When you find out more about Russert and how he achieved his success while keeping his values, you have to ask the question, "Why can't everybody live like Tim Russert?" There is nothing he did that was very difficult. He was very kind. He was hard working. He had all these values that everyone could possess if they wanted to.

From the age of ten, I've been a serious collector of books, mainly sports books. During that time—for the sake of argument, let's call it thirty years—my favorite book style is the "eavesdropping" type where the subject talks in his own words...In his own words, without the 'then he said,' or 'the air was so thick you could cut it with a butter knife' waste of verbiage that makes it hard to get to the meat of the matter. Books like Lawrence Ritter's *The Glory of Their Times* or Donald Honig's *Baseball When the Grass was Real.* Thus I adopted that style when I started compiling the oral histories of the Mike Ditkas and Harry Carays of the world.

There is a big difference in doing a book on Mike Ditka or Harry Caray and doing one on Tim Russert. Ditka and Caray were much older than Russert, thus, they had many more years to create their stories and build on their legends. Furthermore, they both liked to enjoy liquid fortification against the unknown, which leads to even more and wilder tales...and multiple divorces. So the bad news is that when you have someone as straight as Russert, who rarely drank to excess, who was not a skirt chaser, who worked so many hours a day, he didn't have that much time to create stories.

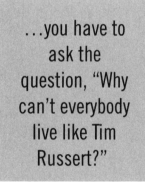

...you have to ask the question, "Why can't everybody live like Tim Russert?"

I don't even pretend to be an author. This book with its unusual format is designed solely for other Tim Russert fans. I really don't care what the publishers, editors or critics think, but am vitally concerned that my fellow Russert fans have an enjoyable read and get their money's worth. Sometimes, the person being interviewed will drift off the subject, but if the feeling is that the reader would enjoy their digression, it stays in the book. So, if you have negative feelings, don't complain to the publisher...just jot your thoughts down on the back of a $20 bill and send it directly to me.

In an effort to include more material, the editor decided to merge some of the paragraphs and omit some of the commas that will allow for the reader to receive an additional 20,000 words—the equivalent of fifty pages. More bang for your buck...more fodder for English teachers...fewer dead trees.

Among the biggest obstacles in putting this book together was the problem with repetition. There was a very similar problem with the Tom Brady book. Sometimes repetition is good. For instance, in a book on Mike Ditka, seven people described a run Ditka made in Pittsburgh the week of JFK's assassination as the greatest run they had ever seen. Yet, only one of those stories made the book. The editor didn't understand that when the readers finished the book, few would remember the importance or singularity of that catch and run, whereas if all seven had remained intact, everyone would realize that that one play summarized Ditka's persona and his career. So, too, the repetition with Tim Russert, except many times greater. It was overwhelming. Almost seventy pages were deleted from this book because there were constant, similar or duplicate testimonials. Even so, many remained.

> ...a man the way men used to be in an America that is not the way it used to be...

It's also interesting—as you'll find in this book—how some people will view the same happening in completely different terms. There was a thought of omitting the attempts at humorous headlines—some of the headlines in this book prove that truly great comedy is not funny—and eliminating some of the factoids since this book was written after Tim's death. But, all of Tim's friends who were questioned in this matter unanimously nixed that idea.

Tim Russert was an unorthodox man in a society where orthodox behavior has stifled creativity, adventure and fun...a society where posturing and positioning one's image in order to maximize income has replaced honesty and bluntness...Tim Russert was a hero, a once-in-a-lifetime person...a principled man in a world of rapidly dwindling principles...a difference-maker on an indifferent planet...a man the way men used to be in an America that is not the way it used to be...a loyal man to colleagues, classmates and friends in an age when most people's loyalties are in the wallet...a man who fought the good fight and lived the good life.

We'll never forget Tim Russert because men like Tim Russert—like memories of people like Tim Russert—never grow old.

Go now.

CHAT ROOMS

Chapter 1

Let's Shuffle Off to Buffalo

One Foot in Childhood and One Foot in Adulthood

CIGAREETS AND WHUSKEY AND WILD, WILD WOMEN

Patrick Hoak

Patrick Hoak was an eighteen-year-old track star at Canisius Prep when he collapsed in a classroom. That's when he found out that he had type I diabetes, a disease he has fought successfully for over forty years. Now working for the Board of Elections in the Buffalo area, Hoak went to Canisius and John Carroll University with Tim Russert.

I didn't meet Tim Russert until we were high school freshmen although we went to adjoining grammar schools. In South Buffalo, there were seven or eight Catholic grammar schools, so one was on top of the other. It wasn't unusual not to meet until you went away to school, so we met at Canisius.

> "…Tim and I… convinced our parents to let us go to New York City…"

To get into Canisius High School was very competitive. They turned down two out of three applicants at that time. It was very expensive to go there—then, it was $320 a year. Although $320 now wouldn't even cover books, back then, it was a big amount.

When Tim and I were juniors in high school, we convinced our parents to let us go to New York City because we needed a rest and a vacation. It still boggles my mind. They bought it, and we had saved our money.

Tim Russert, Jerry Lombardo, Jerry Horrigan, and I went from Buffalo to New York. It cost us $22, round-trip airfare on American Airlines. We stayed at the Statler Hilton, across from where Madison Square Garden is now located. It cost $6.50 a night. Our first night was at the Wellington Hotel. Russert and Lombardo got ripped off in their room from whatever monies they had. Someone broke into their rooms and stole the money. Horrigan and I were roommates. We were quite content there, but they couldn't wait to get out so we had to up it at the Statler for $6.50 a night. Incidentally, the phone number at the Statler Hilton was Pennsylvania 6—5000. That's where Glenn Miller got the idea for his hit song.

We got there and we thought we had a lot of money. Lombardo and Russert's parents wired money to replace what was stolen. We had about $100, which in 1967 really was a lot of money. We're in New York. We were bold. We flashed our fathers' credentials wherever we went. We would go to see Johnny Carson. Horrigan had a press pass from his father for the Bills "Right this way, gentlemen." The four of us got to go right in to see the *Johnny Carson Show*. My father was the state senator. He had just lost his election, but they didn't know that yet in New York. I had his Senate card, and we'd go to Broadway plays as Senator Hoak and his son. "Right this way, Mr. Hoak." Tim's father was a garbage truck driver and a hopper on the *Buffalo Evening News,* driving the news truck. We're having a ball.

Horrigan said after Tim's death, "If you thought we were talking about politics, you're totally wrong...it was all about beers and broads!" Horrigan's brother is in charge of the Pro Football Hall of Fame in Canton, Ohio...His dad was a big shot with the Buffalo Bills.

> "We had invited the pretty girls from the other parties to our party and it was loaded."

There was a party at every floor at the Statler...so we went to all of them. We would pick up beers at every party and take them back to our room...so we could host a party. We've got a bathtub full of beer. At seventeen, we didn't know a screwdriver from a Seven & Seven or a Scotch and water, but we're taking the mixed drinks two at a time and bringing them back and putting them in our room, labeling the drinks so if someone comes in and orders something, we know what we're serving. We had invited the pretty girls from the other parties to our party and it was loaded. We'd go to a party and say, "We're having a party down on the fifth floor in room 520. Come on down." Even at seventeen years of age, we knew we couldn't let people know that was our real age. Being students in Jesuit education, we all had the short haircuts...and we looked about twelve years old. I decided that I was a tenured college history professor from Canisius College. I get this blonde telephone operator from Baltimore Maryland who is twenty-six years old who buys everything I'm saying. We're having a ball. Horrigan gives the details to his female connections. I can't recall the name of who was there, but he had it down like it was yesterday. As the party goes on, it gets to be six-thirty in the morning. Russert comes up to me and Horrigan and says, "Guys, if we leave now, we can catch the seven o'clock Mass at St. Patrick's." I said, "That's a marvelous idea. Why don't you and Lombardo go? I'll stay here with Horrigan and batten down the hatches." ...off they went to church. Horrigan said, "Anyone who would think what a wild, crazy time—whatever you have in your imagination—we still came home sin free." But, our version to our buddies, when we got back...we did everything.

> Russert...says, "Guys, if we leave now, we can catch the seven o'clock Mass at St. Patrick's."

We thought we were wild and crazy and had hit the lottery....

How Tim got elected student union president at John Carroll is still the eighth wonder of the world to me. There were people with money in the school fraternities. Tim was blue collar like most of us from Canisius. We all thought we were above average until we got to John Carroll and found out what those families were making—big money. Yes, my father was a senator, but they made $10,000 a year back then. He owned a restaurant and he was a Buffalo fireman. When they asked for the family income, I lied and said he made $70,000. He didn't make near that much. I was one of two people out of thirty in the class whose parents made less than $100,000. Doctors, lawyers and very well-to-do people.

Tim was an operator from high school right through his life. The one big rule for student union president was you had to bring in top line entertainment. If you get that top liner in, mission accomplished. No questions asked, just do it. So, he comes out with, "I'm thinking of bringing in Muhammad Ali. What do you think?" I said, "That's great, but you're not getting Muhammad Ali." Well, underselling Mr. Russert is not very smart. He got Muhammad Ali...he got the Kingston Trio...he got Simon and Garfunkel...and I don't know how he did it. And, later he got Bruce Springsteen, which wasn't as big of a coup 'cause he was in his early stages, before becoming the superstar he is today. If Tim put his mind to something, he was pretty successful to what he would do.

Tim wasn't as active in sports. He could have played some sport. The Jesuits encouraged us to be on a team. Tim worked high school. He worked for the Jesuits at St. Michael's Rectory to pay off his tuition. I didn't find out until out senior year—why 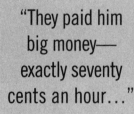 is Tim not in this and why is Tim not in that? About three days a week, he would go to the Rectory, clean it, answer phones, mop the floors—do whatever he had to do. They paid him big money—exactly seventy cents an hour to help offset his tuition. Having to do that really cut into the social aspects—he would have a tight schedule.

"They paid him big money— exactly seventy cents an hour..."

This was when he was on Cuomo's staff. I had gone to Albany every year for several years representing either the town of Hamburg or the Innkeepers' Association of Western New York, which is a group of restaurants/taverns. While I was there, I went to see Tim at his office. I walked in and was asked if I had an appointment. When I said, "No," they told me it would be the next week before I could see him. Tim walked by and saw me. He invited me to come on in. It was quite an impressive sight. All the lines on the phone were lit up. The vestibule was filled with people and there was a line outside the door. He says, "Give me five minutes. I've got to clear the lines." He was talking to Ted Kennedy at the time. He had the *New York Times* waiting on one line and Dick Gephardt on another line. These names stick with you. I can't recall all the other newspapers that wanted to talk with him. He cleared the lines. I said, "I can see you're busy. Let's do lunch." He said, "I don't do lunch." I said, "How about dinner?" He said, "The earliest I'll get out tonight is eight o'clock." Now this is nine o'clock in the morning. This was Tim's work ethic. You'll see how it eventually ties in.

> "I've got to clear the lines." He was talking to Ted Kennedy...

I said, "I can work around your schedule." He said, "Well, go to the Hilton"—which was at the base of this hill in Albany. "I'll meet you in the lobby." I got down there at eight o'clock and sure enough, he shows up. We're sitting there at the bar...behind Tim, a lined formed with people who wanted to talk to him. There must have been twenty people waiting in that line. Tim said, "I'm going to the bathroom. I won't be back. Go over four blocks and there's a little gin mill, The Jug and Barrel. Go in there. It only seats six people. Get a slice of pizza and have a beer. When I leave now, don't follow me. Give me a ten minute head start." Tim leaves. I'm sitting there, and people waiting sure don't want to talk to me. After ten minutes, I get up and leave...and met him down at the bar.

I got back home. It was the Friday after Thanksgiving. I'm opening up the bar. It's eleven o'clock in the morning. A mutual friend walks in. She asked, "What happened?" I said, "What do you mean, what happened?" She said, "Tim got married." I said, "What?" She said, "No, he eloped and went to Spain. What do you know?" I said, "I know nothing." I had no idea.

Tim was a go-getter. He studied hard. Tim was one of the guys who really took things seriously. Tim got his bang out of his love for his education. I'm surprised where he ended up. I never dreamed that he would have been as successful as he was. I felt that Tim modeled himself after Joe—The Buffalo Democratic honcho—Crangle...and, if Crangle did it, Tim wanted to do it.

Crangle was the president of the CYO (Catholic Youth Organization) of Buffalo. The guy who was going to become the new president was Jerry Lombardo, who was on the trip to New York with us. It was a done deal. He was going to be the president, and Russert was going to be vice president, and I was going to be secretary or treasurer or whatever. I never thought twice about this. But, one day we get up, and Lombardo goes, "Tim and I talked it over. I really don't want to be president. Tim wants to be president, and I want to be vice-president." What went on in that bedroom that night...? Tim wanted it because that was part of Crangle's resume. So, Tim became president of the CYO.

> "How Tim got elected student union president at John Carroll is still the eighth wonder of the world to me."

When we had our reunions, Tim would always have a couple of cases of Heineken in his room. I don't remember him drinking Rolling Rock like most people talk about.

Back in 2001, Tim was the commencement speaker at St. Bonaventure University. It's in Olean, New York, which is out in the hills, 90 miles from Buffalo. He was helicoptered in. He had to get back for a *Meet the Press* taping, so they announced beforehand, "Mr. Russert would like to apologize. Normally, he likes to stick around for pictures and autographs, but he is unable to do it because of the tight timetable."

My nephew was graduating that year so my eighty-one-year-old mother, Nora Beasley, was there. I went to a security guard and asked him to do me a favor, "Would you tell Mr. Russert that Nora

Beasley would like to talk with him?" Tim gives his speech and the security guards come over toward us. They are walking Tim out to the helicopter. The guard leans over to Tim and says, "Nora Beasley would like to talk to you." I wish I'd had a camera so I could have gotten a picture of when he turned around and looked and said, "Where is she?" We're up on the third tier. He walks all the way up, sits down with my mother—he didn't care about me—and talked to her for about fifteen minutes, took pictures with the family and with the graduate and with my mother and the graduate.

Meanwhile, Russert's people were trying to get him out of there because of his schedule. Finally, he said, "I'd love to stay, but I really have pushed it too far. I've got to get going." And off he went...much to the chagrin of all the people around us...watching and wondering what the heck was going on. "They tell us he's got to get out of here, and he's sitting here with these people taking pictures!" It meant the world to my mother. Tim was like that. He never forgot her after all those years. This was 2001, and we had graduated in 1968—so this was thirty-three years after high school...and he took the time out to be with my mom. Tim had seen her a couple of times since high school. Sometimes when he was in town, he'd come out to our restaurant and my mother would be there....

> "...ready to try to get Tim canonized... and I knew Tim would be laughing about it."

I was at work here on June 13, 2008. I walked in. A lot of people here knew I had a good relationship with Tim. They came up to me, very white-faced, and said, "Did you hear?" I said, "What?" "Tim passed away." I said, "Tim?" They said, "Tim Russert passed away." I was ashen.

There are so many things coming out since his death about how he helped people. It has really been amazing the articles here locally. They have pictures of Tim running the length of the buses with the caption, "Thank you, Tim." There was another article in the *Buffalo Evening News*, that stated, "Despite high profile, Russert often gave gifts anonymously." Stories about him giving blind people in front of a diner in Washington two one-hundred dollar bills, donating $1,000 for food, scholarships, etc. Russert's second grade teacher said she recently got a call from a Dominican priest whom she didn't know and who didn't leave his name. He was ready to try to get Tim canonized. I was just shocked, and I knew Tim would be laughing about it. But, you know, maybe it's not as far-fetched as it sounds.

WHERE THE PAST IS PRESENT

Paul Cummings

*In 1982, Paul Cummings opened a one-man tele-
communications office in Pittsburgh that quickly
grew under his direction. The former high school
varsity football coach's home sits atop Mount
Washington overlooking downtown Pittsburgh.*

I've known Tim Russert since we were ten years old. We lived
in South Buffalo, which everybody in Buffalo used to laugh
about. They called it a "little Irish ghetto." If you weren't
O'Malley or something like that, people looked at you real pecu-
liarly.

There was a little nine-hole golf course right at the end of my
street and also at the end of Tim's street. Even as kids, Tim and all
the kids would go over there during the summers at night and
hang out and play touch football and whiffle ball and probably
do some things I shouldn't even mention.

We would just cause general mayhem. There was a motorcycle
cop, and, honest-to-God, I think his beat was Cazenovia Park.
You never saw him anywhere else. We thought in our minds—as
teenagers—that his vocation in life was just to harass kids. He'd
ride around on that three-wheeled motorcycle and as soon as
he'd see a bunch of kids, he'd just assume they were doing something wrong and would start chasing after us.

We sometimes tried to get "that cop." Maybe we'd throw water
balloons or stand there while he came up and then everybody
would take off in different directions so he'd have to decide, "All
right, which three guys do I go after?" We knew the shortcuts
through the park. The cop could only go so far and then he

wouldn't be able to go farther on the small, narrow path. Then, we'd reconvene somewhere else in the park. Oh, Russert and the boys loved that.

Tim attended St. Bonaventure grade school, and I was at St. Martin's, even though they were across the park from each other. You probably recall doing the "seven churches" on Holy Thursday. This was a great Catholic tradition that on Holy Thursday you would go to seven churches and pray. It was like a little mini-retreat for everybody. As kids, and being altar boys, which Tim and I were, this was mandatory. You *were* going to go to seven churches. South Buffalo had so many churches in it we could literally walk from church to church. It would be St. Bonaventure's, St. Martin's, Holy Family, St. Thomas and St. Ambrose. We always ended up at the Our Lady of Victory Basilica. He was the monsignor there. He's been beatified, and they're trying to make him a saint. Going there, to us, was the big one—it was our grand finale.

> "...when you came from South Buffalo, people always looked at you with a *jaundiced eye.*"

Tim and I both went to Canisius High School. Canisius is a Jesuit prep school. It was one of those deals where when you came from South Buffalo, people always looked at you with a *jaundiced eye.* It was like they were thinking, "Oh. That's one of those guys from South Buffalo." We used to say that South Buffalo is for the Irish...the West Side was for the Italians...the east side was for the German and Polish...and the north side was for the rich. There were always a lot of kids from North Buffalo back then. Nowadays, it's changed so dramatically, especially with schools closing. Back then, there was always a small pack of young men who would come from South Buffalo—they'd ride a couple of buses and get up to Canisius.

Of course, Father Sturm is still alive. He was the Prefect of Discipline, and everybody feared him. The guy is five-foot nothing. He was a Golden Gloves boxer before he became a Jesuit. Obviously kids knew they were only going to go so far with him. Getting "jug" was Canisius' form of detention after school. Getting "jug" was one thing...having to meet with Father Sturm was something completely different. Everybody watched their P's and Q's around him.

> "Getting 'jug' was one thing...having to meet with Father Sturm was something completely diferent."

I know the story about Father Sturm walking into Messina's Cafe and catching everybody there who'd said it was snowing too hard to get to school, but I wasn't there that day. That was one of the times when we *actually could not* get out of South Buffalo. We heard later about what he did, and the guys around my bus were all going "Thank God, we didn't meet them there." We were actually stuck in South Buffalo. We'd have to leave at seven o'clock in the morning to get up to Canisius. On a morning like that, I think we didn't get into school until ten-thirty or ten forty-five. That was one of our *legitimate* times when we actually did get stuck.

We all became the sports fans just by being in Buffalo. Tim and I used to collect the baseball cards. Then, we'd flip them—that was our form of gambling. We'd flip the baseball cards or pitch them to the wall.

At John Carroll, we were playing for the conference championship in football. Tim would have been a sophomore. We were picked to lose by about thirty points in that championship game. We were up at Thiel College. It was freezing cold—real nasty, nasty weather. These guys were all out cheering for us. We had a huge contingent that had traveled from Cleveland down to Thiel College just to root for the team. We ended up winning the game—something like 38 to 6.

Everybody is celebrating there in the locker room. We're all yelling and screaming. All of a sudden, after I'd taken all of my equipment off and most of my clothes, I'm being carried by a couple of guys, led by Tim Russert, out to where all the fans were congregated outside the door of our locker room. My mom was there, and she yells, "Put him down. He doesn't have any clothes on." I wasn't completely naked, but it was close. Russert loved it.

When we first got to John Carroll, which was a small college, for homecoming and concerts we'd get the B and C of bands. We'd get a band scheduled there nobody had ever heard of. All of a sudden, Tim Russert comes on board and he joins the University Club, which was responsible for coordinating a lot of these big events—spring weekend and things like that. Before I knew it, we had Jefferson Airplane. We had Chicago. We had Billy Joel... before everybody knew him. Tim had this ability. I don't know what he said to these people. I don't know what kind of a turnout he promised them, but we would get these bands. When I first started going there, you'd go to a concert and there's be 50, 80, 100, 200 people there. By the time I graduated, you couldn't get tickets for these concerts. Tim just had this way about him.

I told him one time, after we had graduated, and he had already done very well in the things he had done, "Man, if you had ever gone into sales, you'd be a billionaire by now." It was just unbelievable. When my wife, who had also gone to John Carroll, and I would sit there and watch Tim on TV, we'd look at each other and go, "Tim has not changed." And, here he was fifty-something years old. He was the same Timmy Russert as when he was fifteen, sixteen, eighteen, twenty-two—same personality. Tell it like it was. But, man, could he deliver!

> "He was the same Timmy Russert as when he was fifteen, sixteen, eighteen, twenty-two same personality."

Back when we were kids, it wasn't like Tim Russert, the great newsperson, or Paul Cummings or Joe Jones, the fantastic athletes—it was just a bunch of guys. A bunch of guys hanging out, goofing around, having a ball, laughing, giggling...and always planning the next prank.

I was very happy when I learned that Tim Russert would be attending John Carroll. I was one of the few people who actually played there as a freshman. Recruiting at John Carroll was not like recruiting at Notre Dame. Our coaches typically would say we'd like you to get back to the school to try to pick up some of the guys who might not be going to the larger schools—the Syracuses or Notre Dames or schools like that. We would always try to go after the guys who might be considering a Holy Cross or a Boston University. They were going to be in the top ten. They weren't going to go to Ohio State or go to Notre Dame, but, "Boy-oh-boy, could we use you here."

> "I never did ride in Tim's Gremlin.... That car ran on and on—it just never died."

I was personally recruited at Syracuse, but the only reason they wanted me at Syracuse was that there was another guy on our team who they thought was my best friend at Canisius—we were friends and teammates—but we weren't best friends. They thought by recruiting me, they might get him. My coach talked me out of it. He said, "You're never going to play there. You're going to be fodder." I went to Carroll and although it wasn't a big school, I had a ball.

I never did ride in Tim's Gremlin. But it was hysterical. Remember the Disney movie, Herbie, about *The Love Bug*. Remember what it looked like before all the "magic" took place? Tim's Gremlin was worse! It was like, "How is that thing even running?" That car ran on and on—it just never died.

We used to laugh when we'd see Tim on TV. We'd say, "Here's Tim." He's got the shirt and tie on, but half the time, the tie would be pulled over to the side. His hair always looked like he had just come out of a windstorm. That's the way he looked all the time. And Tim would spill food all over his clothes all the time...and he would just carry on.

My daughter called me within an hour after we heard about Tim's death. I got hold of our great mutual friend, Jace Caulfield. He was actually on his way over to their home at that point, just to see if there was anything he could do to help. He said, "Paulie, Timmy was the same last week when I saw him as he was twenty-five years ago." I said, "Absolutely." You could see it in his tone, in his demeanor, whether it was a public speaking engagement or his Sunday morning TV show. Same thing...a consummate professional. But, he worried about the content. In other words, he wasn't worried that someone might say, "What kind of a suit does he have on?" He didn't care about that because as soon as he started talking, people didn't even notice what he had on. He could have been wearing a pair of jeans and a tee shirt.

That's what he was like at Carroll. There were events where the fraternity guys would have to wear their fraternity jackets and shirts. He still didn't care. He'd have the top button opened and the tie off to the side, and there were coffee stains on the front of it. It didn't bother him because it was the event that was to be in the limelight.

> "You'd better have done your homework when Tim was going to interview you."

Tim could have gone anywhere—number one, because he was smart; and, number two, because he was honest; and, number three, he wouldn't play games. As a matter of fact, between you, me and the lamppost, probably the only thing that could hurt him would be the fact that he wouldn't play games. But I think people would have gotten by that. I still believe that he felt that this is where I'm supposed to be—not in politics—right here reporting it...making sure I dig and dig and dig. I heard a couple of the people who spoke about Tim, and they all said the same thing. He was tough. You'd better have done your homework when Tim was going to interview you. He was never nasty. He was never vicious. He never tried to slant his questions to make the Democrat look good or the Republican look good or the individual look good. He slanted his questions—this is what we're talking about...this is the issue...what's your stand?

Our social life in high school and college was great. We all enjoyed ourselves. We went out. We did all the things that typical high school kids did. You've got to remember that when we were back in New York state, the drinking age was eighteen, which means, obviously, that by the time we were fifteen or sixteen, if you could put a quarter on the bar, you could get served a beer. There was a place not too far from school called Maxl's Tavern, which was an old German kind of beer garden. They served hot roast beef sandwiches on Kümmelweck rolls. It was about two blocks from school, and on any given Friday afternoon, you could see any number of kids from Canisius down there. Just as likely as anybody else, you might see Tim Russert, not necessarily the big shot in school government or the big shot in whatever

"...Father Sturm would show up... the manure would hit the ventilator."

and not the big jock, but absolutely one of the guys, and he could fit into any kind of crowd. If it was a bunch of football players sitting in there, he'd walk in, and it was like he played on the team with us.

Occasionally, Father Sturm would wander down to check it out...and the manure would hit the ventilator, especially when there was a dance at Canisius. A lot of us would tell our parents we were going to the dance, and we'd take an extra buck or two. We'd go to the dance, get in and then meander down to Maxl's. We're sitting there having a roast beef sandwich and a couple of beers, laughing and giggling, telling stories....every once in a while, Father Sturm would show up and absolutely...the manure would hit the ventilator.

Tim was one of the guys who was like, "I'm here, too, Father." He wasn't sneaky. He wasn't conniving. There were a number of guys who might typically try to sneak out the back door so as not to get caught, but most people who knew Father Sturm knew he'd find out if you had been there, whether you snuck out or not. I'll tell you what, if you snuck out, and tried to get around his wrath, that was worse. The Jesuits are tough. They are great educators and they're tough, but the one thing they will absolutely not tolerate is deceit and lying. It just turns them. Ironically, most of us who came out, we talk about the same thing. When any group of us get together, it's the same thing. I talk about it in business all the time. I say, "I've been managing people. If I find out you're cheating on your expenses, that tells me you're cheating somewhere else, too." I think that's one of the things—not just from Canisius High School, but from John Carroll because it was the same there. Getting caught doing something was one thing, but getting caught doing something and then trying to lie about it and say you didn't—a big no-no.

> He always thought of, "Okay, how do I get this accomplished?"

Tim wanted to make his family better. He wanted to make the people around him better. He wanted to make his job better. Other people are so concerned about the "what if's?" What if I can't do it? What if I'm not successful? What if I get fired? What if that girl doesn't like me? Tim never thought in those terms. He always thought of, "Okay, how do I get this accomplished?" Even though he probably didn't realize it when he was sixteen, eighteen, twenty-two years old, that's the way he acted.

His attitude was 'I choose to do it because I know it's the right thing to do.' Tim was impeccably prepared for his weekly shows and any interviews he was doing. One of my buddies told me a story after Timmy died. He said that very, very close friends of theirs were having their twenty-fifth wedding anniversary, or some occasion like that, and were having a party on a Saturday night. Tim almost never did anything socially on a Saturday night, just because he had to fine-tune, get ready and be well rested for his show. The wife of this couple asked Tim if he would go. She said, "I know you don't like doing things on Saturday night, but this is a very special night. We're just having a dinner party. It's a very small group. Would you please come?" Tim and his wife went. He didn't have a drink. He socialized for a little bit, had a bite to eat and thanked them both and out the door he went. They both understood that he had to go. Ninety-nine folks out of that one hundred would have said, "Well, this is a special occasion. I can party tonight." It just wasn't Tim's way. He knew that he couldn't do it. He knew that wasn't part of his strategy. He wasn't rude to them. Obviously he showed them the respect of coming over, spending a little bit of time, having a soft drink, socializing with some very close friends, but then, "I have to go now."

> "Tim almost never did anything socially on a Saturday night, just because he had to fine-tune, get ready and be well rested for his show. "

Very rarely, maybe three or four times three or four of us did ride together back and forth to South Buffalo. Not too many of us had cars. When we found out that somebody did have a car, whether they borrowed their parents' car or whatever, and that they were going back to Buffalo, sometimes there would be six or seven people in a four-passenger car. That three hours and twenty minutes that it took to get from John Carroll to South Buffalo just would fly by. Everybody had their own little pockets of friends and little pockets of situation that were going on. The stories would just fly...before we knew it, we were pulling off the Thruway to South Buffalo.

Sunday morning, some would get together and find out what time they were leaving. Most of the people were hung over from Saturday night. There was always this, "I've got a paper to do," or, "I've got this or that to do," so we grudgingly would meet somewhere and hop in a car at two or three o'clock in the afternoon and fly back.

Hearing Tim talk about Buffalo would bring on the warm and fuzzies. It was one of those things—you'd hear him and you'd think, "He's talking about my town." It was always said with such enthusiasm and sincerity that you knew it wasn't some guy with the attitude, "I'm from Buffalo so I'd better say something nice about it." Tim meant it. Buffalo was his town. Hearing it would give us the chills.

When his first book, *Big Russ and Me*, came out I got it and read it and just laughed and would tear up. You'd be reading and then, "Oh, I forgot about that. Now I remember." Hearing him tell the stories about Father Sturm or about Canisius or about this or that. It was always like, "Oh that's right. I forgot about that." It brought back the things that had happened thirty or forty years before.

Another reason why people liked Tim so much: He didn't do all the things he did to get popular. He didn't do it to get wealthy. He just did it because he wanted to, and he had this burning desire to get all these things done. His goal wasn't to be a millionaire, and it wasn't to be the most popular newscaster on television. It was because it was a great job and he could do something for someone. Timmy truly believed that what he did in his job helped to impact people. And he did.

> "Hearing Tim talk about Buffalo would bring on the warm and fuzzies."

WHEN THEY GOT ALL THE WAY BACK UP TO BROKE, THEY THREW A PARTY

Jerry Lombardo

After graduating Canisius Prep with Tim Russert in 1968, Jerry Lombardo entered the Jesuit seminary in Poughkeepsie where his only visitor—outside of his family—was Tim Russert. Six months later, Lombardo dropped out and entered the University of Detroit, from which he graduated in 1972.

Just before our senior year, we had gone to New York City on a trip together. We came back, and he announced that he would run for the next CYO diocese president. At the time, I was going into the Jesuit priesthood. Tim was the only one I confided in that I was doing that until graduation day. In my yearbook, he wrote, "Year 2000, Tim Russert-President of the United States; Jerry-Pope Jerome." We did Boys State together. I had been in the Jesuit seminary for about six months and Tim was the only one who visited me.

> ...he wrote, "Year 2000, Tim Russert– President of the United States; Jerry–Pope Jerome."

CYO was very, very big at that time. It was the major Catholic social organization. Tim and I had come into it, and they had their hierarchy of people who would succeed. In New York City we had the idea Tim would run for president; I wouldn't. The whole idea that we were so powerful as high school students that we would be the ones to name it, rather than the adults who were in charge of the organization, was pretty heady.

When he became CYO president, Tim proved himself extremely well. He gained a real respect for the establishment and they had a great respect for him in terms of what he was able to do. The following spring, I went into the Jesuit seminary. Meanwhile, Tim and I each won the Monis Christi award. It was a major award for a young person. He was a recipient and I was a recipient. Tim had to intervene for me to come home for the award presentation because the Jesuits wouldn't release me. My parents had no idea we were getting the award, but Tim made personal arrangements for my parents to be at the Buffalo Statler Hilton at this banquet in their Gold Ballroom. This was a huge event. My parents heard my name announced, and they went up to the front with me. My mother is the only one still alive, and she still talks about that moment. Tim helped arrange that moment so my parents wouldn't miss it. He was that kind of a guy.

> "Tim helped arrange that moment so my parents wouldn't miss it. He was that kind of a guy."

In fact, when he visited me at the seminary in 1969, it was Super Bowl Sunday. Joe Namath was the quarterback for the Jets. It was the first year the AFL won a Super Bowl. It was time for dinner and the Jesuits were put out by him, but they couldn't say anything. He refused to come to dinner and insisted on staying to watch the game, in which the Jets went on to victory. When it was over with, Tim came in to dinner. Tim was that kind of a guy but he had a personality so they couldn't get mad at him. They wouldn't agree with him, but they still enjoyed him. I don't remember Tim being on any teams in high school. CYO was a major, major organization. That occupied a great deal of his time.

There was Tim Russert, Jerry Horrigan, Pat Hoak and myself. The four of us went off to New York City the week before our senior year when we were seventeen years old. I was the youngest of the four, but the largest of the four. This was a PG-rating of our own awakening in terms of what life is about. It was the first time we were without our families and out of Buffalo.

We stayed in a hotel. Our first night was at the Wellington, which was a real dive. When we went out, Tim left his wallet in his room. He came back and discovered his money was missing. We moved out of there and moved down the street to the Statler.

We grew up in a time where there were all kinds of benefits for being a youth. At the Statler, we had two rooms, both studio rooms. Tim and I shared a room and Jerry and Pat shared a room. We paid about $7 a night, each. Everything was considered half priced. We went to New York with $125 and stayed an entire week, and that was air fare, a hotel, our meals and our entertainment. We all came back with change in our pockets. That was a great experience we had there.

In New York at that time, the drinking age was eighteen. I would be the one who would be sent into the places to buy the six-pack. Their birthdays were all in the spring, and I had a summer birthday.

We had planned our trip to New York all that summer. Each one of us went to our parents with "Mr. and Mrs. Russert said that if I could go to New York, Tim would be allowed to go." And "Mr. and Mrs. Hoak said...." I don't think we ever talked to any of them, but all four of them gave consent. I remember Pat Hoak's father said, "Now, listen, you can do some things there that you could regret for the rest of your life, so you make sure you make some good decisions." All four of us came back with a real respect for our parents and, although we were definitely teenagers, we felt like we weren't going to violate their trust. We weren't going to do anything that would embarrass them or bring any kind of shame to anybody. Don't forget, my mom is still alive. We went to Mama Leone's, which was a very well-known Italian restaurant. It was a cellar restaurant. You could get these cheap meals with huge amounts of food. You'd get these five-course meals, and it only cost $5. You had soup, a side of pasta, and the main course. We went down there

> ...Tim kept telling the waiter, "I only want spaghetti."

to eat, and Tim kept telling the waiter, "I only want spaghetti." The waiter said, "Yes, we'll give you that, but what do you want to order?" Tim said, "I only want spaghetti."

I also remember when Tim got a driver's license. He'd come pick me up on the weekends. One day we drove from Buffalo to Syracuse and had dinner at a Holiday Inn restaurant and then went home. The whole idea was that he'd just got his car and he wanted to put it on the road. He said to me, "Let's go for a ride." So I said, "I'm game for it." Here we go... three hours away...have dinner and go home. Tim was like everybody when you first get your license—you're willing to run every errand there is around the house.

> He said, "That's what I am—a man of the people—available and accessible to everybody."

One time he was working out of the New York office and wasn't in Washington yet. I called his office and said, "This is Jerry Lombardo. Is Tim available?" I was put right through. He said, "Hey." I said, "You're supposed to be one of these most important people, and you just take your calls." He said, "That's what I am—a man of the people—available and accessible to everybody." We just talked and reminisced about different things. I said, "Hey, you never showed up at my wedding." He goes, "You never invited me." I think there was something there where he wondered why he didn't get a wedding invitation...and I wondered why he wasn't there. In talking with him, all was fine. Tim was that easy to talk to, even these many years later.

In high school, we were very good friends because we shared some common interests. I was reading in some of my yearbooks where he wrote, "I owe you a lot socially and academically. I'll see you at Boys State. We should have a good time there together." Tim never had any one circle of friends. Tim seemed to find a place with all kinds of people. It wasn't like he had a clique and that's who he stuck with. He definitely socialized with a lot of different people. As much as he had his feelings about how things should be done, he also knew how to respect different points of view. The guy who was the moderator for CYO at the diocesan level was a big heavy-set guy who wore white shirts and black ties and argyle socks. We were in penny loafers and sockless. Most people would look at the guy and just make judgments. I remember during the year Tim said, "You know, Mr. Arby, he really has a lot of good thoughts. He really cares about us." That was just the kind of a guy Tim was. He'd be the first to have an impression or to say "I'm going to do it this way," but he had no problem respecting another point of view and saying, "Hey, it's just as legitimate. Just because it's different, it doesn't make it wrong."

> "He got as close to the White House as anybody else I know."

I AM NOT A CROOK

Ellen Crooke

Ellen Crooke has risen fast through the ranks of NBC affiliate news directors. In late summer of 2008 she left WGRZ-TV in Tim Russert's home town of Buffalo for an even bigger job in Atlanta.

In South Bend, I was the news director at WNDU, the NBC affiliate on the Notre Dame University campus. We had heard that Tim Russert was coming to speak at the university. This was right after the election with the white board. Tim was somebody everybody wanted to be speaking with.

We were very excited that he was coming to South Bend. Out of the blue, I got a call from him—from him directly, not a secretary, not a middleman. He left a message saying, "I'm going to be in town if you want to do promotions or interviews." Well, of course we wanted to. I called him and left him a message, and he called me right back. He was so kind.

He was running late, and we had brought everybody in to do a few promotions. The whole crew was in. Somebody from Notre Dame called and said, "We're sorry. Mr. Russert is running late, and he won't be able to come." We were all just heartsick. I started to send people home.

I had given Tim my cell phone number. About ten minutes after we had gotten the call from Notre Dame, my cell phone rang. It was Tim. He called me "Chief." He said, "Chief, don't worry. I know what it's like to lose an interview. We'll be there. Don't you send anybody home. I'm coming."

I thought he was so kind and so nice to go to the trouble to do that. He could have easily just let it go. He walked into our newsroom. This wasn't planned or anything, but there was an automatic standing ovation because everyone was so appreciative of him making the extra effort.

At times, he would send a note. One time, he sent a *Meet the Press* hat. He sent a regular personal note to thank us. He was so kind. I just wondered how he had the time to do that.

The next time he came to South Bend, I was leaving for Buffalo. I had just taken a job to come to Buffalo. He could not have been nicer. He gave me ideas on how to cover Buffalo. He gave me his understanding of Buffalo. He went out of his way. He barely knew me, yet he seemed thrilled for me. He seemed so excited for me.

When I arrived in Buffalo, there was a package waiting. It was a note from Tim. I have it framed on my desk. It says, "You will love Buffalo and its people." /s/ Tim Russert. It was just amazing to me that Tim Russert would take the time to do that.

> It was a note from Tim.... "You will love Buffalo and its people."...

Later, Tim was starting his book signing tour. Again, he—not his secretary—called me and explained the book he was writing and that he was going to do a tour. He would like to come through and asked us if we would do interviews. He came and spent a lot of time with us. There was a luncheon. It turned out that I was with him for a lot of the morning between interviewing at our station and the luncheon at The Buffalo Club. Everybody was having their book signed. Then, I got back to my office, and I thought, "Oh, no. I never had him sign a book." I felt so bad for doing that. I got a phone call from the front desk telling me that there was a package down there for me. He had left a book there for me, signed, "To Ellen, my friend and colleague." For him to take the time to do that—I will never forget it.

This was at the time when our station in Buffalo took on a mission that we're the station that will ask the tough questions and hold the powerful accountable. Tim loved that. It was in the winter and all our reporters were wearing red coats. We put multiple reporters on one particular story. The community started calling us the "Red Coats." Tim heard about that, and he thought that was the greatest thing. He would call from time to time and say, "Chief, what are the Red Coats doing? Are the Red Coats on a story?" He was like a kid, proud of our little station and that he was a symbol for us. He's the symbol of holding the powerful accountable for us. He thought it was great that we were doing that. The last note I got from Tim said, "Go Bills...and go Red Coats." He loved it that much.

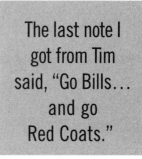

The last note I got from Tim said, "Go Bills... and go Red Coats."

Tim Russert was someone who had so much to be proud of. He was brilliant and successful in what he did, but he took great joy in making other people feel proud. He'd meet people and he'd say something to them about being proud of something. He really took pride. I think that's why he looked at Buffalo, and he wanted Buffalo to feel good about ourselves. He wanted somebody to be rooting for them...to be rooting for the underdog. That was the spirit he had. To me, that was remarkable coming from somebody that successful. He seemed to take such joy in making someone else feel proud.

I work for Gannett and had been at Gannett meetings in Washington on June 13, 2008. I was returning home and had just landed in Buffalo and gotten to my home. My newsroom knew what he meant to all of us and to me, so they called me. His death had not yet been released to the public. We were very careful. We didn't want to be the first to report it because we knew his family was here and we knew that they hadn't told Big Russ yet. Right after he had collapsed, we got a call. Then, they called me at home. I remember calling the people I knew in Washington, "Where are you hearing that? Are you sure?" We just didn't want it to be true. We waited until Tom Brokaw made the announcement before we did anything, to even go out into our neighborhoods because we didn't want his family to find out from us.

Our newsroom rallied so much over that week. It was very important to us to cover his story with justice. I said to people, "Why did this happen?" I've seen a change in journalists since this happened. The journalists whom I work with seem to be kinder, to make an effort to help people, and also to ask the tough questions, holding people in power accountable. It made us think twice about that. I know, too, that one of the things we've done here is we've established an award in his name within our newsroom. It's called the Tim Russert Award. Every two months—the first one was at the end of August—people will be nominated by their peers for the award. There are two criteria: 1) to have conducted an interview that you were completely prepared for and in which you asked tough questions, an interview that really makes a difference, or 2) to have helped someone in our newsroom—to have taught them a skill or helped one of your peers within our newsroom. Tim's quote that we all were so impressed by: "The greatest exercise for the human heart is to bend down and lift someone else up."

"The greatest exercise for the human heart is to bend down and lift someone else up."

If there were a reason that God took Tim at his age, maybe it was because of how he lived his life. That could be a shining example for people, and I really think it has been. I really think people have taken to heart how Tim lived his life. Not just how great he was as a journalist, but how he lived his life.

Maybe the reason God took him was so that a life could be shown. If he had retired in his seventies from *Meet the Press*, there'd be, "Oh, he was great," but not so much the life that he had led would have been shown. I think the fact that he was taken so young made us all want to learn about him more and hear what his life was like. It was so shocking that it got everyone's attention.

I know of no other network person who came close to treating the affiliates like Tim Russert did. Tim Russert was so thoughtful of all of us. He was willing to do whatever we needed. He would help at a moment's notice. No one else even remotely compares. I think that's why, when Tim walked into a newsroom, people were so enamored with him...and he seemed to be genuinely enamored with us. He loved to hear how things were working. He didn't come up like other network journalists who had worked in a small station. He came into the business in a different way. He was always fascinated with how everything was done: "Where do you find talent? How does this work?" He took great joy and passion in

> He was always fascinated with how everything was done: "Where do you find talent? How does this work?"

learning about other people, and not just letting people know about himself, which you see so often in others. This business is filled with egos because your career can change on a dime. People have to always be trying to prove themselves, but Tim became successful by lifting others up. That's an amazing difference.

When you read Tim's books and read his life story, you find he came from humble beginnings. One article I read which I felt was true talked about his upbringing. So many people do come from humble beginnings like Tim. He lived an average life. There was "something" in Tim. Listen to Sister Lucille, who was very influential in his life. We interviewed her and realized there was something about him from the moment he was born that was special. The fact that he didn't come up wealthy and privileged—that he had to work for it was always in the back of his mind. I truly, truly believe that that it was rooted in his Catholicism.... If you look at what he did, and I think about this all the time and teach my kids about it, he was somebody who lived the Ten Commandments. Honor thy mother and father. What did he do the last years of his life? He talked about it all the time. He said it to me personally. He wanted to honor his father and the life of his father. He truly was living out the Ten Commandments.

Among the famous and powerful—who else lives their life that way? That dichotomy is just something you don't see anymore.

I cannot tell you the number of people who've said to me, "I've never been so affected by the death of somebody I never met." People felt as though they knew Tim Russert. They felt as though he was our greatest ambassador. They know Buffalo is a wonderful place. If you live here, you love it. But, it's also a place that's misunderstood and that has gone through tough times. Tim Russert was our ambassador. He was the one rallying us, helping us to feel proud about where we live. We felt as though we lost our ambassador.

> "Even the people who hadn't met Tim felt as though they had lost their friend."

I was honored enough to have met Tim Russert. Even the people who hadn't met Tim felt as though they had lost their friend. I've never seen it like that. Just a few weeks prior to Tim's death, a man who had been our mayor for sixteen years passed away— the longest-running mayor in the history of the city of Buffalo. Not to take anything away from him, but there was nowhere near the pain people felt then as when they realized Tim Russert was gone.

There are famous politicians. But what's interesting—it wasn't about what Tim did professionally. It wasn't about the stature Tim had reached. What it was was how he treated people individually. I can't get over how many people he touched like that. That's what made his death what it was. Yes, he was in the national spotlight, but he lived his life touching so many people individually and being so kind to people and helping people. There are so many of these stories that just amaze me. I don't know anyone else who lives their life that way.

Perhaps the lesson is—why doesn't everybody live their life like this? Perhaps that is Tim's legacy—to make people want to live a better life. It was not just for his journalism, not just professionally, but how to *live* a better life. Who else do you know who has made it up to such a powerful position who unabashedly reminds people every day...and people loved that.

The last meeting I had with him in my office was for his second book tour, *Wisdom of Our Fathers.* He was being interviewed during our six o'clock morning show. He came early and we were sitting in my office and talking. I had a White Board—just like his—that we plan things out on. I remember looking up, and he was staring at it and reading what was on it. It was not any political information or anything. My daughters had been in my office the night before, and they had written doodles on it: "You rock, Mom." "Love you, Mom." He looked at it and said, "You know, Chief, that's what life is all about. You should be so proud that your daughters would say that to you." It stuck with me. It made my year when he said that. What a thoughtful man!

> My daughters... had written doodles on it: "You rock, Mom."...Tim looked at it and said, "You know, Chief, that's what life is all about."

IF FOOTBALL'S A RELIGION, WHY DON'T THE BILLS HAVE A PRAYER?

Jack Kemp

Jack Kemp ran for the Republican presidential nomination in 1988 and was Bob Dole's vice presidential running mate in 1996. He served in the United States House of Representatives from 1971 to 1989, representing the Buffalo, New York area as a Republican. In his seventeen-year pro football career he played quarterback for the Buffalo Bills and was the American Football League's Most Valuable Player in 1965 after the Bills' second AFL championship. He was captain of the Bills and also the San Diego Chargers. He currently serves on corporate and nonprofit boards and remains an active political advocate and commentator.

I got to know Tim very closely when he was with Senator Daniel Patrick Moynihan, who was a good friend, albeit of a different party.

I think Tim went straight from Moynihan and Cuomo to NBC. If I remember correctly there was a big dispute over the Fair Housing Law, which, incidentally, this is the fortieth anniversary of the 1968 Fair Housing Act. I remember making this a big issue 'cause I like to think I was a Republican who believed very strongly in civil rights. I made fair housing one of the key elements of my tenure at HUD, which was strongly supported by Senator Moynihan. There was a dispute in upstate New York. I can't remember which town it was but there was a fair-housing dispute. Tim contacted me on behalf of Senator Moynihan, and we worked with both Tim and Senator Moynihan with good results. It was done expeditiously and it was resolved to the benefit not only of the law but of the people of that town.

Tim was a tremendous aide to the Senator. It certainly gave me a great respect for Moynihan because it was a very vexing challenge to HUD on how to adjudicate this problem without having to go to the Supreme Court or go into court.

Tim and Al Hunt, who then was with the *Wall Street Journal,* and their wives Maureen Orth and Judy Woodruff, and Joanne and I were friends and friendly. When Moynihan passed away, Tim and some others had a party, a recognition dinner, for Patrick Moynihan and his wife, Liz. Tim Russert asked me to give the Republican perspective on Moynihan because I felt he really was a senator who was above partisan politics in many ways.

Tim and Al asked me to make a toast and give some remarks about Moynihan. Of course, I added some old Tim Russert stories and Al Hunt stories. They were good buddies and both of them used to tease me to death about politics and economics and capital gains taxes and enterprise laws and just about everything I ever did in Congress.

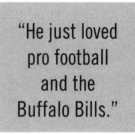

"He just loved pro football and the Buffalo Bills."

Every time I saw Tim, he called me "Old number 15 Kemp", no matter where I was. I could be on *Meet the Press.* I could be on the streets of New York. I could be at NFL Commissioner Paul Tagliabue's office. We all went down to see Commissioner Tagliabue. Senator Chuck Schumer, Tim Russert and I met with Tagliabue and Roger Goodell about keeping the Buffalo Bills in Buffalo. Every time Tim went to talk about me, he would say, "Old number 15", and he'd always have a big smile—a big Irish grin on his face. He just loved pro football and the Buffalo Bills.

Tim was one of the biggest sports fans of any public figure. And I don't think the Bills had a bigger fan than Tim Russert. I loved the idea of them naming the highway that goes to Orchard Park and Ralph Wilson Stadium after Tim. That's just frosting on the cake, as far as I am concerned.

Tim had an encyclopedic mind, not just about the Bills, but about professional football, the NFL and sports in general. He had that great sense of humor about the old Buffalo Bills, as well as the Jim Kelly era. Tim was just a down-home, genuine, wonderful encyclopedic sports fan.

Moynihan—and this is strictly the view of Jack Kemp—is from the Scoop Jackson, Hubert Humphrey, Harry Truman wing of the Democratic party. He was pro-defense. He favored U.S. foreign policy. He certainly was a strong, strong anti-Communist Democrat, again, like Scoop Jackson and Hubert Humphrey and Harry Truman. He was a great supporter and defender of the State of Israel, all of which are views that I hold firmly myself. I consider Moynihan to be one of the great patriotic politicians of the twentieth century. Russert learned a lot from the senator.

I think you can elevate Moynihan, Scoop Jackson, Hubert Humphrey, John F. Kennedy and Harry Truman into that great tradition of a bi-partisan foreign policy, which also comes from both Everett Dirksen, who believed in enacting the Marshall Aid Plan, and Moynihan. Moynihan was just a giant of that tradition. He was one of the greatest ambassadors to the UN, where his name is revered by men and women who care about those issues that affect, not just America, but the cause of freedom around the world.

> "...I don't think there was a fairer interlocutor on TV than Tim Russert."

I never heard any rumblings of Tim Russert running for public office so it's not in my experience to say that I ever heard him suggest a desire to run for office. I never thought that. He was devoted to journalism and despite his partisan Democratic background, I don't think there was a fairer interlocutor on TV than Tim Russert. He was the "gold" standard of fairness and objectivity and a desire to get the truth. He would always put up your past statements...and he'd make you defend it. He wouldn't just ask a question, he would allow you to answer it. And he wouldn't just let you answer it, he would follow it up. So many journalists on TV ask a question, and then they jump to a totally unrelated question. With Tim, he established a premise, questioned you about it and went at it, tooth and nail, so to speak, until he had fully flushed out your views as well as his desire to put you on the spot. I really appreciated, in this age of what some people call drive-by journalism, Tim was one of the few journalists and interlocutors who gave you a chance not only to answer the question, but to give him a chance to ask a second and a third and a follow-up question. I found Tim Russert to be among the best ever.

FROM THE FIELD OF SCREAMS AND THE LAND OF AHS

Mike Buczkowski

Mike Buczkowski has been general manager of the Buffalo Bisons for twenty-one years. The Bisons are the Triple A minor league affiliate of the Cleveland Indians.

For the last ten years, we would ask Tim Russert to send us a video that we would use on opening day on our JumboTron. The video board would open up and say, "This is Tim Russert." Then he would talk about Buffalo and about the ballpark, and he would actually say, "Here are your 2008 Buffalo Bisons." Each year on Opening Day, that's how the Bisons took the field, with Tim introducing them.

> "…on Opening Day…the Bisons took the field, with Tim introducing them."

We would just call Tim and ask him to do it, and he would do it. Most of the times, it looked like he had done it right on the set of *Meet the Press*. He probably did it right before or right after the taping of the show. He would do a minute or so video and would send it to us. Tim did this for us at no charge.

Tim came a couple of times to throw out the first pitch at the season opener. The time people remember the most was a couple of years ago when we did "Tim Russert Day" here. We had worked with him on designing a bobblehead—a Tim Russert bobblehead. I have to admit that this bobblehead does actually look like Tim. It looks pretty good. The bobblehead shows Tim with a Bison hat on while wearing a suit and tie.

At different times, we had done bobbleheads for some of our more popular players and our mascot. We wanted to do something a little bit different from a player bobblehead. We were thinking—who from Buffalo would people really enjoy getting a bobblehead of that would be a collectors' edition, something really unique? It didn't take us long to arrive at the name of Tim Russert. We just knew that he would be the one. We didn't know if he would do it. It was just incredible the way he embraced it. He just loved the idea. He thought it was the best thing going. At first, we were concerned that he might not want to do it. Not only did he want to do it, he wanted to help design it. He had some of his own ideas for us. Then, he said he wanted to come in for it. So, then we had to decide how to schedule the day. We scheduled it on a Sunday when there would be an

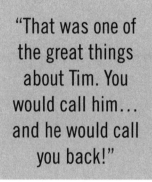

"That was one of the great things about Tim. You would call him... and he would call you back!"

afternoon game. He had some taping to do early that morning and flew up from D.C. for the game and got here not too long before the gates opened.

My family had known the Russert family forever. My mom's family lived a couple of doors from him in South Buffalo. The bobblehead concept came right after the famous wipe-off board election. Tim had been through town, and we had sent him things over the years. Obviously, he's got a connection to baseball in his book. He talked about his son, Luke, being partially named after Luke Easter, who is a famous old Bison player. We had the idea. I called him, and he returned my call. That was one of the great things about Tim. You would call him...and he would call you back! You didn't have to talk through five different people to get to him. He asked about my mom and the family and how everybody was doing in South Buffalo.

I said, "I have an idea for you" and proceeded to explain the idea for a Tim Russert bobblehead doll. "What do you think?" He said, "I think that would be a great idea. Let's do it. That would be

Courtesy of Buffalo Bisons

great. I'll come in for the game, and we'll do a whole day." That happened about a year in advance that we started planning the day. Tim was very involved in the design of the bobblehead. He would say, "I've got an idea. What if we do this? How about if we do it this way?" It was funny. I would get these calls. Tina, my assistant, would come out and say, "Tim Russert is on the phone." He'd say, "I've got another idea for the bobblehead. How about if we do this?" He actually came up with the design—the bobblehead is holding a white wipe-off board. Instead of it saying, "Florida, Florida, Florida," it says, "Buffalo, Buffalo, Buffalo." We gave those away to the first 5,000 people who came through the gate that day. This all happened right after his first book had come out.

In the making of the bobblehead, first you take several pictures from different views and send them to the manufacturer. Then they make an actual mold. They make up the mold and ask how it looks to you. You approve it and then the next thing you get is a picture of the mold that has been painted. You look at the eye color and other aspects of the coloring. You approve that. Then it is ready to go into production. Every time we got a new step for approval, I would send that to Tim so he could be in on all the decisions. When the painted mold came, he made some more suggestions. Then, we had the finished product.

The bobblehead is one of the top draws in baseball giveaway days. We had to move ours to one gate to try to control the crowds because it would be chaos. People would come through the gate, get their bobblehead, and then they'd want to go another gate and say, "I didn't get one." So now we only do them at one gate.

People will be lined up an hour before the gates open to get these bobbleheads. They quickly became a collectors' item. I believe way back in the 60s, bobbleheads used to have a special allure, and then it seemed like they got away from it. Like everything else, they came back into style. People collect them. If you go on eBay and type in "bobblehead," it's amazing what you'll see.

When we gave away the Tim Russert bobblehead, people were lined up even longer than an hour before. I think that day we drew 12,000-13,000 to the game, and we gave away 5,000 bobbleheads. It was unique. Before that, we had done our mascot and had done former players, so it was the first "celebrity-type" person that put a Bison hat on and did the bobblehead. He told me, "I have it on my desk."

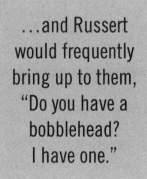

...and Russert would frequently bring up to them, "Do you have a bobblehead? I have one."

Afterward, Tim mentioned to me that he would be talking to people important in Washington, the other party would be describing something neat that had just happened to them, and Russert would frequently bring up to them, "Do you have a bobblehead? I have one." So, he had fun using it talking to very influential people in Washington, and he'd say, "Yeah, but do you have your own bobblehead? I have my own bobblehead."

On Tim Russert Bobblehead Day, Tim brought his dad, his son, his wife, and his sisters. I think we had pretty much the whole family here for the game. He threw out the first pitch with his dad, Big Russ, and his son, Luke.

Then, Tim sat in the concourse and signed autographs, took pictures with people, and people even brought up the bobbleheads for him to sign. We were supposed to be down there doing this for thirtu minutes on the concourse, and he ended up being down there for about ninety minutes. I kept asking him if he was okay, and if he wanted us to cut off the line, and he said, "No, don't cut off the line. I want to see everybody." He ended up staying down there for a long time signing autographs and talking to people. It was great.

> "When it came to Buffalo, it would never have entered Tim's mind to charge for signing the autographs…"

When it came to Buffalo, it would never have entered Tim's mind to charge for signing the autographs and doing the pictures with people and making an appearance. On the national stage, he was our best spokesman. He was incredibly proud to be from here. He was not shy about telling anybody where he was from…writing about it…talking about it. Sports is such a huge part of the Buffalo community, so there's a natural connection there if you're from Buffalo with the Bills, the Sabres and the Bisons. I think Tim felt that. He talked about going to Bisons games as a kid with his dad and seeing Luke Easter at Offerman Stadium which is where the Bison played at that time. He talked about those being some of his best memories from his childhood.

Tim Russert was a knowledgeable baseball fan. When he would call me, he'd say something like, "I was looking at the standings in the paper. It looks like the Bisons are making a run." He knew who we were affiliated with. Obviously, he didn't get to too many games, but he talked so fondly of the days as a kid going to Bison baseball games.

We won the International League Championship in 2004. One of the other things I remember that he did on the national stage was doing one of those interviews with Matt Lauer on *The Today Show*. Tim was not with Matt in the studio, but they were doing the interview by satellite. Russert finished talking about the key political time coming up and he said, "Matt, one more thing. I have to congratulate my hometown Buffalo Bisons. They won the Governor's Cup last night in Buffalo, and it's a great day for the Bisons." We didn't have to call and tell him the Bisons had won the championship…he knew.

Every time Tim would say anything about the Bisons, it was great. Here's a guy who, first of all, is much loved in Buffalo. He doesn't have an enemy in Buffalo. Tim was such a great guy, and then, to find out nationally that he was just as revered. People respected the job he did and everything he put into being a professional journalist and broadcaster. Also, to find out that Tim did count-less other things like this around the country, whether it was charity or other things he did to help people. You heard all the stories after he passed away, about all the things Tim did. When you have a well-respected national figure talking about your minor league baseball team back home, it made you feel proud. It made you feel that the Bisons were getting good publicity and that Tim really cared about it.

I remember the day he was here for the first pitch. He was doing interviews. He was talking to people. He's here with his family. He's singing *Take Me out to the Ball Game* in the seventh inning. In between, he's taking phone calls. He's obviously talking back to Washington about plans or news. He just made time to do all this stuff, and I think he

> "...it was just incredible to see that Tim was just like a regular guy."

generally enjoyed it. We've dealt with a lot of different people over the years who come to ball parks—famous people to throw out first pitches, or people who sign autographs, and it was just incredible to see that Tim was just like a regular guy. He didn't expect any real special treatment. He wanted to meet people. He wanted to thank people for buying the book. He wanted to greet "Mrs. Smith," who he probably knew when he was a kid in Buffalo. He enjoyed talking about Buffalo, and he enjoyed being back here.

On June 13, 2008, I was sitting at my desk and got an e-mail alert of breaking news. I remember opening it up, looking at it and thinking, "This can't be. This isn't the real Tim Russert." My first thought was that it was Tim's dad because his dad is older and the reports have been that his health was not great. I remember looking at it again...and looking at it again...thinking, "How can this be? This can't be Tim Russert." I turned on the TV and nobody had a report for a little bit. I remember thinking that it had to be a mistake. Hopefully it's a mistake!

Nowadays, you can go right onto the Internet and do a search. I did that...and, sure enough. There it was. Then it came on TV so you knew it was for real. It was surreal—hard to believe.

I think if you understand where Tim came from—South Buffalo—it's a very tight neighborhood—Irish-Catholic—kids didn't have a lot growing up. Like many of the families in that area, you learned that how to get by is to make friends and keep friends and to be loyal to people and to help people when you can. In later years, Tim, a lot of times, just couldn't believe the good fortune he had. He reverted back to those days when you shared good fortune. In that neighborhood, if there was a family who had something and another family who needed help, you helped. It might be helping their kids get a job or help with dinner or if a tragedy struck a family, everybody pitched in and helped people get by.

> "When Tim Russert threw out the first pitch, his son and his dad were involved."

In a lot of ways, we've lost that "neighborhood feeling." Neighbors aren't as close to each other. South Buffalo is still one of the neighborhoods that is pretty much intact in Buffalo. Back in those days, you didn't move out of South Buffalo. You grew up there. Maybe you bought the house down the street from your mom and dad. Or you moved upstairs. You probably married a girl from South Buffalo whose family was from that area so the neighborhood stayed connected. Unfortunately, in cities like Buffalo, a lot of times now, when cities run into hard times, young people move out to find jobs. There wasn't a steel industry anymore where thousands and thousands of people were employed. There were always jobs to be had. That has contributed a little bit to the fact that neighborhoods are just not what they used to be.

When Tim Russert threw out the first pitch, his son and his dad were involved. We had jerseys for the three of them—Bison jerseys with their names on it. They came down to the dugout, they talked with players, they did interviews. He didn't practice much for that first pitch. What they ended up doing, they all three went out to the mound. Big Russ started out holding the baseball. He handed the ball to Tim. Tim handed it to Luke, his son, who actually threw the pitch. You could see that the three of them were very close, just in the short amount of time, I was able to be with them all. They sat in the dugout. We got great pictures of the three of them. Luke is very personable. I think he enjoyed the day when he was here. He didn't have that same connection to Buffalo Bison baseball because he didn't grow up here. His dad was always reminding him, "We have Luke Easter's jersey number retired— he's one of only three that we have retired." The three are a guy named Carnegie, who played for a long time in the '30s, Easter #25 and Jeff Manto #30. I remember Tim pointing out saying, "There's the guy, Luke Easter, that's the guy."

Tim did our Opening Day video again this year. After Tim passed, the next home game, we had a short ceremony on the field—a moment of silence. We had pictures and video clips set to Bruce Springsteen music. We knew that Tim loved his music. It was a video-look at Tim Russert's visits to Buffalo and especially to the Bisons. We played the video one more time. We call it the "run-out" video. It's the video that the players run out onto the field to. We played that one more time. There were a lot of tears. Obviously, all the local media were here. People came that night who had met him. Some people brought the bobbleheads. He had given a few *Meet the Press* hats out to people. People wore those hats that he had signed. A lot of the crowd were people who came just to remember Tim.

"It was a video-look at Tim Russert's visits to Buffalo and especially to the Bisons."

My mom was part of an organization called South Buffalo Live, where they helped beautify the small parks in the neighborhood. They had contacted Tim, who donated money and helped revive a few places, so they were naming a children's park after him. This was when he was writing the book. He would call my mom and ask, "What was the name of the family again who lived around the corner who had the six kids? I want to make note of it in my book." He would call her to help check on some of the stories he was going to write about in the book.

> "Not only did Tim show up, but he ended up being the keynote speaker."

Tim was close to my Uncle Paul. They were very close in age more so than my mom. My Uncle Paul passed away several years ago from the effects of the Vietnam War. He remembered my Uncle Paul. Mom contacted Tim telling him they were going to do a memorial in D.C. for people who died as a result of the war—not actually died in combat, but they were going to be adding those people to the wall of the Vietnam Memorial. My mom and grandmother were going to D.C., so she contacted Tim. Not only did Tim show up, but he ended up being the keynote speaker. He talked about the war and mentioned my uncle and my family. That's just the kind of guy he was. He showed up there—Paul was his friend—so why wouldn't he show up?

Opening Day at the baseball park next year will be strange not to have the video of Tim. He had been the one to do it for the past nine years so it will be very different.

These days, we even have a tough time getting some of our players now to sign autographs. They're AAA minor league baseball players. It's like pulling teeth to get some of them to come out and sign autographs for a while. Then, you have a guy like Tim Russert—and it was a hot day—who sat in that concourse, stayed right there, shook everybody's hand, took pictures, signed autographs for hours.

WHY CAN'T SUGAR BE AS SWEET AS FATHER STURM?

Fr. John Sturm

Father John Sturm was the Prefect of Discipline at Canisius Prep High School when Tim Russert was a student there. He is still active at the age of ninety-one and is just finishing up a trilogy of books. The first book is titled Life's a Dance Without a Dress Rehearsal. *The second book is* Let's Dance With Life. *The third, which he is working on now, is* Your Responsibilities in Life. *A former student at Canisius High School many years ago, Father Sturm was very familiar with all the tricks the students tried to play on him.*

Tim Russert came to Canisius High School from South Buffalo. The kids from South Buffalo were cocky and tough. As a result, I tried to split them up, not only so they wouldn't create more trouble, but also so they could enjoy the Canisius students from other parts of town.

Tim Russert had a nice personality and a wonderful wit. His eyes were eager to get moving. He didn't want to sit still. He never liked to sit still. It was almost like he had too much energy for his own good. When he came to us, he had been an editor of a grade school newspaper, which had helped develop his skills. He was always doing extra-curricular things, which he continued throughout high school. Most kids don't have that much energy. If they do, they spend it in less positive ways than Tim. He had a truly positive attitude and was a joy to be around *most of the time.*

Early on, one of Tim's first few weeks at Canisius, I caught him sneaking a sandwich out of his locker during classes. I put him up against the locker. Russert thought I was going to hit him, and he said, "Father, have mercy." I told him, "Russert, mercy is for

God. I deliver justice." Tim quoted that statement many times over the years.

I think Big Russ was responsible for much of Tim's attitude. His father was a hard-working man, and Tim became a hard-working man. Big Russ taught his son to know the way to do things and to always do them the right way—never cut things short.

I know that the Russerts, like many other families, made great sacrifices so that their kids could go to a parochial school and get a quality education. I was surprised at how much success Tim achieved. When you looked at him in high school, he was friendly, but you never thought he would reach the incredible heights that he did. On the other hand, I guess you never think anyone is going to reach those heights. When you teach students, you guess what is going to become of them. Some will be successful in arts, some in business—you haven't given much thought to it. Successful men tend to change their way of life and their patterns so you can never predict how they will turn out. Sometimes the biggest goof-offs in high school end up being the most successful. You have hopes for all of them, but you don't really know. That's the great thing about being a teacher: helping mold them and then watching them develop.

I told him, "Russert, mercy is for God. I deliver justice."

When you're head of disciplinary matters in a school, you get a sense of the tenor of the class. You begin to sense that something will take place because you hear the kids talk or you've seen kids do the same thing before. As you go along, you just know something is about to happen. You have to put two and two together.

One of my favorite Tim Russert stories, along with his other cronies, involves a blizzard. There are always big snowstorms in Buffalo. The kids from South Buffalo had to switch buses downtown. One time, Tim calls me and tells me that he and his buddies are trying to get to school, but it doesn't look like they're going to make it. I could hear noise in the background and knew that they were probably at Messina's Coffee Shop, which is a restaurant right near where they had to switch buses downtown. Russert goes on and on about how they're going to try to be there and how awful it was and the buses weren't running and everything else. I smelled that one because I'd seen it before. I go down to Messina's and when I walked in, there are Russert and his buddies, Jace Caulfield and a few others. They looked like they had seen a ghost...I mean their mouths fell open...they were scared! I marched them all back to school and gave them "jug," which is detention. They all hated jug. They couldn't stand jug. I gave all of them two weeks, but Russert had a job answering the switchboard down at St. Michael's rectory. He said, "Father I have to be at St. Michael's." I said, "Good, then you can serve it over a month or two, but you 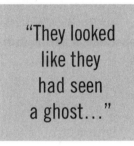 have to serve the detention." If you read the history of any Jesuit high school, jug is detention after school. Instead of calling it detention, most Jesuit schools call it jug. It's the first three letters of a Latin word, jugum. A lot of people think that jug stands for Judgment Under God, at least that's what a lot of students like to think it was. During jug, the students would have to write essays on any subject I might think about at any particular time: "Raindrops on a window," or "How do you put a shine on a sneaker?" Things of that nature would cause them to use their imagination. I'd ask for 500 or 750 words. I don't remember any specific essay anyone wrote and I never kept them. The Jesuits have been educating students since 1400. Peter Canisius was a great German leader in Europe and established university after university. He also established a method of teaching according to the principles of St. Ignatius, the founder of the Jesuit order. It was adapted through the years and all the Jesuits had the same sort of spirituality and knowledge so they put it into practice in the classroom.

All these kids always thought they were coming up with new inventions for getting away with things. They didn't realize that, not only had I been a student and had seen it from the student's side, over the years of being Prefect of Discipline, I saw it all. Now, I don't know if I ever got Russert in this situation, but there was an old burlesque theater downtown, also not very far from where they switched buses. It was called the Palace Burlesque Theater. As these students got older, they oftentimes would try to sneak their way in there. I befriended the ticket sellers at the Palace. Lots of times, these kids would be so naïve, that they would walk up to the ticket window with their Canisius letter sweater on or something that would identify them as being Canisius students. Lots of times, the ticket-taker would give me a call and describe the students.

Other tricks I would do is I would get on these buses—not at school and not where they switch buses downtown, but somewhere along the route at other stops the buses make. I was trying to check to see if the Canisius kids were smoking or maybe were trying to smuggle a beer or whatever. They also used to sneak into a place called Maxl's and try to sneak beers there. I've been told that there were a lot of hasty exits out the far door when I walked into Maxl's.

"…there were a lot of hasty exits out the far door when I walked into Maxl's."

Overall, Russert was an excellent student with no real disciplinary problems. But, I did nail him good that day at Messina's.

Tim and I talked frequently, usually not for very long because he was so busy. I would call and congratulate him on the show or question him as to why he did this or why he did that. Most of the time, it was just to say, "Nice going."

The biggest change in students today from the time when I was in school and the time when Tim Russert was in school is the lack of respect and the inability to take responsibility. There are some exceptions, but these are general characteristics. It's not really their fault…they're not taught it by their parents. Society doesn't teach them at all. Life swings back and forth like a pendulum. The younger generation—what's happened to them will change because they won't want their kids to be like they were. They know what happened to them.

Tim Russert was well liked and respected by people on both sides of the political spectrum because he was so honest and truthful. People aren't used to hearing the truth. I was always proud of Tim and his success on *Meet the Press* and on MSNBC. Like any teacher, when you find one of your students has really been successful, you are proud of it, and you always claim it as your own.

> "He was a great representative of Canisius, of Buffalo, and of everything that's good."

I've enjoyed my life. I've made some mistakes, but they've all made me become better. We learn from our mistakes. I was in my room here when Tim had the heart attack. Someone called the pastor of St. Michael's shortly after it happened. Then the pastor called me in and told me to sit down, that he had bad news for me. He said, "Tim Russert just passed away." I said, "You have to be kidding." He said, "No. I would not kid about a thing like that." I just couldn't believe it. We'll miss him dearly. He was a great representative of Canisius, of Buffalo, and of everything that's good.

CULTURAL LEARNINGS FOR MAKE BENEFIT GLORIOUS RUSSERT NATION

P. J. Griffin

P. J. Griffin grew up next door to the Russerts and attended the same schools K through College—seventeen years with Tim Russert. After graduation from John Carroll University, Russert headed off to law school and Griffin entered the teaching profession.

As a kid growing up with Tim, he always needed to win. He knew the rules. When there would be an argument about a play, Tim always won because he knew the rules, no matter what we played.

When we played basketball in the back yard, he'd know some vague rule—he must have gone to the library and read books and gotten these rules. All the rest of us would do is play. He'd call something and we'd all yell at him, "What? What are you talking about, Russert?" "That rule is such and such, such and such." And he'd be right.

In the winter, we played a lot of hockey, but we never had skates. We'd have three on three or four on four, and we'd play in the street. We didn't have the kind of goals kids have today. We had two "snow mounds" that would be our goals. We put magazines in our pants and tied them up with either duct tape or with an old sock or something like that underneath our pants so they would be our shin guards. You couldn't see them, and we played in our boots, just running up and down the streets, checking each other into the adjacent snow banks. We would have sticks and a hockey puck. When a car came, we'd have to scoot off to the side. The car would pass, and the game would resume again. We played this when we were in eighth grade through our sophomore year in high school. When we were old enough to drive a car, we weren't interested in playing street hockey. We were into other things— bad things!

We would get a lot of snow and schools would be often closed for several days at a time, which was to our delight. We would sled, of course. Also, we would hitch rides on the back of cars, which was illegal. We'd hide at a stop sign and two or three of us would jump out and grab the bumper, duck down low into a catcher-like position and get a nice little ride for a block or two. Tim was in that all the way with us. We called that "hitching rides." He liked to do that.

Tim Russert played sandlot baseball, but he didn't play for the schools or universities. He was a scrappy, tough little sandlot player. He had other things on his mind. His agenda wasn't what ours was. He knew what he wanted to do long before most people know what they want to do. He was involved in politics and communication. He was real good at it. We'd be having a ball game down in the park on the sandlot. We said we'd all be there at two o'clock...but Tim wasn't there. He was maybe down at Democratic headquarters doing some kind of work they needed him to do. We were all just playing ball. He was focused and knew exactly what he was doing, even in high school. He was way more focused than we were. Politics were a passion with Tim. I grew up dreaming I could become Mickey Mantle. He grew up dreaming he could become John Kennedy. He had goals that none of us saw. We were all trying to be ballplayers and superstars, and Tim was going a different way very early on.

> "He was a scrappy, tough little sandlot player. He had other things on his mind."

Politics was truly number one for Tim. When it came to sports, this guy was different there, too. He knew the rules. He knew batting averages. He knew pitchers, ERAs. He knew things we didn't know. We all liked the Yankees. Tim liked the Yankees, too...but here's why he liked the Yankees—Yogi Berra was doing this and

Mickey Mantle was doing that and Roger Maris.... He knew batting averages. He had scores. He had earned run averages. He had all that stuff down—he had it down. He was one of the most thorough individuals I ever met in my life for knowing his stuff. He really knew his stuff.

"Politics was truly number one for Tim."

When Tim got to college, he became a student government pervert. He was student government president when Kent State happened. Kent State was just down the street from John Carroll, which is in Cleveland, Ohio. He was very distraught over it. I met with him and he said, "We're closing down the university." We all had finals to take, but the Kent State massacre happened and they just thought it wiser. He was adamant in that. He dealt with the administrative staff, spoke to them, and then sent out the word to the rest of the student body that we were going to close down.

I LIKE IT, I LOVE IT,
I WANT SOME MORE OF IT

Frank Szuniewicz was my brother Dennis's godfather. Frank was about twenty years older than Tim Russert and was Deputy Controller of the city of Buffalo. The year after Tim graduated college, he and my uncle worked together and shared an office. My uncle really liked Tim because, for a young guy, Tim was really into politics and knew politics well. My uncle was into politics, fishing, smoking and playing cards. He would often ask Tim how long he was going to be at this job. Tim would say, "I'm going to be here until I get enough money to start law school." My Uncle Frank said, "Well, how much money do you need?" Tim said, "I'm about $2,000 short." As a result of that, my uncle was afraid that if Tim stayed around city hall too long, he would never go to law school. He knew that law school would be very helpful to Tim's future and felt that Tim, of all the young guys he'd ever met in his life, had a really bright future in politics. Later that summer, after a particularly good night of playing cards, my Uncle Frank loaned Tim Russert $2,000 in cash, probably in small bills from money he had won in the card games.

Frank's Grill was a bar my uncle owned. It was a neighborhood hangout and was also a Democratic party grass-roots type of hangout. My uncle at first was the Water Director of Buffalo. Then he got to be Deputy Controller. He was always involved in politics. Everybody used to get together at Frank's Grill, and that's where he won the money in card games.

After the book *Big Russ and Me* came out, Tim Russert had a book signing here in Buffalo. I went down to it and was standing in this long line. When I finally got up to the table where Tim was, I teased him and said, "That $2,000 came from my uncle, and my father probably lost a lot of the money you got." I thought Tim was famous for his sense of humor—he didn't have any that night. He said, very straight-faced, very seriously, "I paid it back."

At first I was taken aback...so much for his sense of humor. Then, as I thought about it and reflected about it, I think he had a sense of humor, but not when it came to his integrity, not when it came to what was important to him. From his background and our background, you pay your bills. You walk ten miles to pay back a dollar. So, he didn't have a sense of humor then. It was a strictly business and a friendship deal. Frank loaned Tim the money. Tim didn't forget it. He couldn't wait to pay him back. My uncle, I think, refused to take interest on the money.

I don't think Tim ever got in those card games because, at that age, he probably couldn't afford to, plus, they didn't like the young guys. They wouldn't let me play when I was about that age—twenty-one or twenty-two. I remember that there were always piles of money on the table—just piles of money on the table. I could easily see how my uncle made that $2,000. But it could be true...that if my uncle never loaned him that money, Tim Russert may never have gone to law school and would never have been involved with Senator Moynihan, Mario Cuomo and everything else that he did. My uncle is long gone now. He died of lung cancer from all the cigarettes he smoked, but he was very proud of knowing Tim Russert and of his small role in helping Tim get to such a high level.

—CHERYL SZUNIEWICZ, Buffalo

Tim was three years younger than I. I was the paperboy when Tim helped to deliver the papers. This was back in the '50s in the Kennedy era. We both lived on Woodside, which was a middle-class type area. I had the paper route, and Tim lived about five houses down from me, so he helped me deliver the *Buffalo Evening News*.

Tim was a big John F. Kennedy fan, as were my parents and most other Catholic families on the street. Most of us went to Holy Family Grammar School, which was about a mile from our house. We all walked back and forth every day.

There were many, many kids living on our street. We used to go to a place called Morgan Park and play baseball. One day, I just asked Tim to help me deliver my papers. I was a little older than most of the kids on the street so I coached them in baseball.

Back in that day, you didn't play at night, and your parent. wouldn't have been able to come to a ball game. They were working. Tim's father had two jobs.

Everybody knew Tim was an honest type of guy. He wasn't trying to pull anything over on you. I didn't do any adult things with him. My association is all when we were kids—baseball players, collecting baseball cards, trading baseball cards, paper route.

On my paper route, I would occasionally pay him a dime to deliver my papers for me so that I could stay over at the park and play baseball. One time, I found him putting John F. Kennedy flyers into every copy of the *Buffalo Evening News*. He had gotten these flyers from another paper boy, and he was inserting them into all the papers because even at a really young age his family, like all families in our neighborhood, were big JFK fans. I caught him doing it and asked him what he was doing. He told me he was putting these flyers into the newspapers. I told him, "You can't do that. This could cost me my job. You can't do that. This is just a newspaper." He said, "So what?" I said, "Either stop doing it, or I'm going to lose my route, and you're never going to get paid a dime again." He never did it again; he understood money.

—BILL CLOUDEN, 61, Trinity, Florida

My recollections of Tim Russert go back to the '60s until his death. Tim never changed. He was always an outgoing, vivacious, enterprising individual who wore his love for his family and his city and his country on his sleeve.

I first got to know Tim when we were both involved with the Erie County Young Democrats back in the '60s. We were all part of Joe Crangle's Young Democrats. We got to know each other then, and then we knew each other in Albany when Tim worked for Cuomo and I was a state senator. We played softball together. We dealt with state business together.

Tim unabashedly boosted Buffalo at every opportunity he could. Back in the '70s, when late-night talk hosts like Johnny Carson, were making fun of Buffalo because of the weather, Tim Russert became a very credible counterbalance to national pundits who would make fun of our city. Tim took the opposite course, boosting Buffalo through supporting its sports teams and its people and its communities. Through Tim's book and his national presence on TV, he was able to use his clout to upwardly enhance the people and the community of Buffalo, New York.

Tim was the keynote speaker at the National Conference of Mayors in January of 2004. He got up in front of 1,000 mayors and talked about me. He said his friend, Tony Massiello, who is mayor of Buffalo, was in the audience. He went on to talk about what a great country America is because two sons of sanitation workers in Buffalo, Tony Massiello, son of Dan Massiello, and obviously, Tim Russert, the son of Big Russ, had been blessed with success. One became mayor of Buffalo and the other became an NBC news and television correspondent. Tim said, "That's what America is all about." That made me feel very proud, to hear Tim recognizing our fathers and also the fact that in America, you can make it regardless of where you come from.

There's no question, Tim was a Democrat in his heart, but he certainly was unbiased in his ability to quiz and probe government officials and politicians from all walks of life.

There are a lot of clichés that have already described Tim, but he made no secret of his love for family and church and community and America. I know that Tim never changed.

In Buffalo, New York, back in the '50s, '60s, and '70s, Buffalo and Erie County had a very strong Democratic organization headed up by Joe Crangle. Joe basically had a farm system. He would start young guys like Tim Russert, me and many others who went on to elected office, we would be the young guys and gals who would put up the signs, hand out the literature and drive candidates who ran for office, and then he would keep moving these people up as they got older and more experienced. We really learned from who I thought was the best political strategist in New York State, Joe Crangle. We all came out of that farm system.

Tim was such a genuine, real and honest person that news, politics, government and TV all needed someone of his honesty and integrity.

—TONY MASSIELLO, retired mayor of Buffalo

When I was going to law school, I worked for the Department of Streets on the afternoon shift. I worked on what we called the Ashcan Garbage Office. Tim Russert's father was the foreman of that route. I got to know Mr. Russert 'cause I had to deal with payroll. Then, I later became county chairman and he asked me to help his son with a job. I had him working up at Democratic headquarters. When Pat Moynihan ran for senator in '76, I had Pat agree that if he were elected he would open a Buffalo office.

Tim was very engaging, hard working and very balanced. Things never went to his head. He was a real good plugger and came up with different thoughts. He didn't ever try to elbow anybody out of anything.

I'm certainly most pleased that he did so well. Given the background, I can understand it 'cause he never lost that basic touch with people and the really ordinary, extraordinary things of life.

When I heard that Tim Russert had died, I was in my office and just couldn't believe it. I still find it very, very hard to believe. It's hard for me to comprehend that he's gone. He was only in his fifties. My mother used to say that "only the good die young."

—JOE CRANGLE, noted Buffalo politician

After we graduated, I was tending bar at a couple of different places. Tim would come in. Tim and I just had a casual relationship. We were never that close. The fact that we were both from Buffalo was the bonding agent. Other than the unpublishable fraternity parties.... In fact, I didn't even know that Tim had gone to Woodstock. Creep that he was, he didn't tell anybody! If you've seen pictures of him with his Fu Manchu, he was the typical college student, very politically active. We knew he was going to be a politician of some sort from the get-go. He was always working the room. The bond he had with his dad is another thing that a lot of us didn't know.

Russert was good at supporting our teams at John Carroll. He was my biggest fan. He was always there. After the games, we'd get together. Sometimes we'd travel back and forth to Buffalo.

—JIM BOLAND, Buffalo native, JCU football player,
owner of a Goodyear tire store

I was two years behind Tim at Canisius Prep High School in Buffalo. As a freshman, we were never allowed to speak to upperclassmen...or they'd kick our butts. Canisius was an all-boys Jesuit prep school. The upper classmen were always pulling pranks and stuff on us.

Tim Russert was the vice president of student council. He was on the debate team. He would always book the bands for our dances in high school. I remember that he booked Springsteen at John Carroll University, which is his big claim to fame in college. He was always on one student committee or another. He was always that guy in the hallway handing out literature. He would be up in the library on Career Night.

I last saw him at a Cubs game a few years ago. I did the whole "Hey, Canisius" thing. We talked briefly. I bought his books just to read about my home town and my high school and trade stories about Father Sturm, our prefect at discipline.

I grew up in the 'burbs and would bus in. He was a city guy. There was a big difference between the suburban guys and the city guys. The city guys seemed to appreciate it more. Tim got the *most* out of that Jesuit education. He talked it up big time. He talked up the city of Buffalo. Talked up our high school. Talked up his way of life. I was so proud to be able to say, "I'm from Tim Russert's home town. I went to his high school. I lived that life. And I'm in the same business." I was so proud of him that it was unbelievable. Tim Russert had a huge forum.

Phil McConkey went to our high school and played for the Giants and won a Super Bowl ring. Anthony Yerkovich wrote *Hill Street Blues* and *Miami Vice*. There were a lot of writers. Mark Russell, the political comedian and commentator who was frequently on PBS with his piano and political bon mots. There's a whole list of people—doctors, lawyers—it's just really a testament to that way of living and that style of education. It was all about discipline. You're pretty much encouraged to play a sport, and it was mandatory you play an intramural sport and have some activities going on other than just going to class. There are a lot of things wrong with the Catholic Church and a lot of things wrong with the

Jesuit Order and everything else—I don't want to get into that—but back then, it was a great, structured way to get an education.

I was at work when I found out Tim had died. I just stopped in my tracks—I was stunned. I'm fifty-six, this is happening every week now. It is very disturbing to me to lose childhood heroes like Jim McKay and Charlie Jones, then Russert—it's just one after another. Tony Snow was fifty-three. Just "Stop!" Stop it. My best friend has cancer. He just got laid off by FOX today. Today's another bad day for me.

The reaction to Tim's death was such a wake-up call for all of us in our business. We get so immersed in this stuff. To see him drop dead in a minute and end his life—you've got to enjoy life outside of this business.

Also, the reaction to his death was absolutely incredible. It was as if he were a president. It showed you, on both sides of the aisle, every one genuinely liked and respected him. He's a guy who always did his homework. He ate books. He ate research.

—MARK GIANGRECO, sports anchor, WLS-TV Chicago

Tim and I attended high school together. Tim was president of the CYO, which would be for fifteen to eighteen year olds from the counties of western New York. I was involved with that as well until we graduated from high school. When we were kids in Buffalo, there were seven or eight or ten, many of which are closed. Two major rivals, Canisius, where we attended, being the Jesuit school, and St. Joe's, the Christian Brothers school. Those were the two top schools and the two that have remained. There are a few others that didn't close, but we baby boomers pushed our way through. Typically four or five of the top students from the elementary schools would end up at Canisius. Tim and I were there and, for the first few years, we were definitely small fish in a big pond, surrounded by guys who had lots of money and lots more status than we had. Tim's niche was that he was one of the guys, which, in high school, is the greatest compliment you can pay somebody. He didn't stand out by being a sports star or debate star or chess star—he was one of the guys. Those of us who were one of the guys appreciate that in each other. CYO is where he started to show the leadership skills that clearly he took with him through the rest of his life.

I knew Tim was a Bills fan when we were kids. We've talked a little football over the years. Tim stood out. Maturity is not the right word, but there was just something about Tim. If there was silly or crazy stuff going on, Tim was removed from it—detached from it. It was clear that his mind was working in a different direction. Some guys stand out and they're ghouls or dorks—the kind of guy you want to slap around 'cause they're different. That wasn't the case with Tim. He was one of the guys but there was something about him that was just a little different. He was going somewhere. It wasn't that he was arrogant about it. It was something *we* perceived.

—RAY ORRANGE, 58, professor, University of Buffalo

Chapter 2

John Carroll University:
When Cleveland Calls,
Ya Gotta Accept the Charges

Mom, Dad Send Money!
Tuition Just Went Up $2 a Case

IT'S HARD TO CHEER
WITH A BROKEN HEART

John Marcus

John Marcus is the glue that holds the John Carroll Class of 1972 together. He is swamped as the class secretary when he is not working his consulting magic.

Robert Beaudry went to John Carroll years ago. He was a leader, went to Georgetown Law, and died in a plane crash. Both John Carroll and Georgetown had the Beaudry award. Timmy won it at John Carroll. It was a prestigious award in that you're cited as the top dog in the class. Tim was always busy, always working, always campaigning, always talking to people and glad-handing. He always had that smile on his face. He was always busy, busy, busy. You never saw him sitting still.

Tim had designs on what he was going to do in the future, and he followed it. *Rolling Stone* magazine did an article on Tim way back in the '80s talking about how ambitious he was. He was, but what young man isn't? Damn right he was ambitious, but in an absolutely great way. He was a leader just by nature. It was so natural to him to do that. In the very beginning, he was campaigning for freshman class president, shaking hands and meeting people. Tim was never phony. He was always attentive to your needs. He always said "hello." We laughed. Because there are certain images. When Tim wrote the speech for Cuomo in '84, they cut to a side shot showing a profile of Cuomo, and you could see off in the wings—there was Tim standing there with his arms folded, rocking back and forth. That's what he always did—never sat or stood still. You'd see him rocking forward and back, forward and back, and you'd laugh. They had some reporter from D.C. who was out covering the wedding of one of the Kennedy kids in Hickory Hill where Ethel Kennedy lived. There in the background is Russert walking through the crowd. He's carrying a bottle of beer, but you knew it was Russert the way he walked.

When Tim was on Imus and other entertainment shows, it was all about laughter with him. He loved a good story, loved to laugh. At John Carroll homecomings, Timmy's room would be Action Central. One day Jim Peters, a John Carroll Hall-of-Fame basketball player, and I were walking into Murphy Hall, our dorm. I said, "What in the world is that noise?" We walked down the hall, and there had to be fifteen guys in Russert's room, telling stories. You would laugh just listening to them laugh, not even to have to hear what was being said, It was so important to Tim to do that.

Tim was well liked when he was at John Carroll. I never felt people were jealous of him. Tim was just above everything. The only reason you wouldn't like someone would be because of their personal manner or their personal beliefs. And personality—everyone liked Tim. He was a hard guy not to like. He 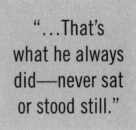 was a big Irish guy who liked a good story. He was smart as hell. Those eyes—he's got those inverted eyebrows that showed passion—would just drill into you. You couldn't get anything past the guy—never could. He was very, very smart...and wise. He was street-wise, too.

There were sixteen of us from John Carroll at Tim's funeral. Afterward, they had the reception at the Kennedy Center. We went downstairs into the opera hall, which was packed. It was a private affair—by invite only. There was every mover and shaker in Washington—everyone from Alan Greenspan to Newt Gingrich—Democrats, Republicans, print journalists, TV journalists—everyone was there. It was unbelievable.

I'm with these John Carroll guys, and we've always been a pretty grounded group. That's the thing that was so important for how grounded Tim was. That's what everyone talks about. I'm standing there with three of the Carroll guys—Jace Caulfield, Tim's close friend was one of them. We went up to the rooftop where they had four bars, one in each corner of this 100-yard long reception hall—totally packed. Everywhere you looked, you saw people whose faces were familiar—Kennedys, Shrivers. I asked someone, "Is there another bar that people don't know about?" He said, "Go down to the left." Sure enough, there was a bar with nearby doors opening out to rooftop terrace. I said, "They got their drinks. I'll bet you they're out there." There they were. The Carroll guys are sitting there, and they all have Rolling Rocks in their hands in honor of Timmy, sitting with the St. Alban's classmates of Luke's. The Carroll guys introduce themselves to the all those guys sitting there, and I said, "Let's have a toast to Big Red." I swear to God, as soon as I said that, a double rainbow came out. I said, "Look at that." I had never seen that before. It's the old Irish tradition of a pot at the end of a rainbow—I've never seen a rainbow end. The nearby rainbow dropped into the trees exactly next to the Lincoln Memorial and splashed purple, red, yellow—all the colors of the spectrum onto this one tree next to the Lincoln Memorial. I'd never seen that before. We're sitting there experiencing this magical moment. Luke walked up to us and we all say hello and express our condolences to him. He goes, "Where's Bergy?" All of a sudden, Marty Bergerson walks up, and he and Luke hug like he's a long-lost uncle or something. Bergy is a guy with unbelievable stories. He certainly is the most colorful member of our class and it has nothing to do with his red hair.

> "The nearby rainbow... splashed purple, red, yellow—all the colors of the spectrum onto this one tree next to the Lincoln Memorial."

We were all in shock. Tim was our superstar. We had NFL coach Don Shula at John Carroll—he's our other superstar. Everybody has captains of industry and guys who run hotels and have big jobs making tons of money...but Shula and Russert were our two superstars. There was such a sense of shock because we all lived through this guy. I don't think anyone would not admit to that. All of us told people, "I went to school with Tim Russert." It was a source of immense pride for us.

Christians wear things that say, "What Would Jesus Do—WWJD." I keep thinking, "What would Tim do?" For the next three weeks, I found myself thinking that. Tim was such a moral barometer for us. We would laugh when people said Tim was ambitious. Yeah, he was. So? He was ambitious...and he was grounded—I always wanted Tim to run for President of the U.S.

I didn't know it until after his death, but Tim had been asked many times, "Why don't you run for office?" His answer was, "I've got the best job in the world. Why would I want to do that?"

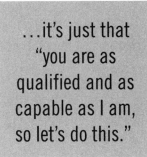

...it's just that "you are as qualified and as capable as I am, so let's do this."

I found it interesting, almost a little selfish, that someone who, as a voter and as a political consultant, I can look at and say, "This guy would be fabulous." He could speak. He was engaging. If you remember back when...I'm a huge John Kennedy fan...JFK mobilized the country. He made us feel like we could do it. "Ask not what your country can do for you—ask what you can do for your country"—is much different from the policies they are advocating today. Tim would have been all about rugged individualism. It would have been, "I worked on a garbage truck; why can't you? I published my own newspaper when I was in eighth grade; why can't you? I put myself through John Carroll University; why can't you? I put on a Bruce Springsteen concert, some unknown rock guy, to put myself through a year at Cleveland Marshall Law School; why can't you?" It's not, "I'm better than you," it's just that "you are as qualified and as capable as I am, so let's do this." That's what Timmy would have been doing.

As for his winning the presidency, my side, the Republican side, would have killed him. Tim had so much on record for what he advocated and stood for. We would have had a field day in research...He had such sensitivity for those who less fortunate, but it's like a child. I think that if you coddle and spoil a child and give them whatever they want, you're going to get a monster. As a society, this country was founded by people who said, "I'm going to a better place, and I'm going to create a better world. I'm going to get my chance to work." We're getting away from that with many people—it's not socialistic, but socialistic tendencies certainly. You pander for votes. You pander to a bloc to get the votes, to bring them to your side, and maybe not do the right thing. Maybe Timmy had seen politics from the inside out, and he probably was smart enough to say, "I can do more keeping these people on a moral plane than I can in a political office and have to make my deals," because he would have been forced to make deals. The NRCC or the NRSC is recruiting, the same thing with the DCCC. Another John Carroll guy, from the class of 2000, I think it was John Powers, is running for congress in Buffalo. He's an Iraqi war vet. He was getting courted and it was all about how much money he got. This kid decided he would take on Tom Reynolds, former chairman of the NRCC, for the war stance. He started the race and DCCC said, "Yeah. Let's do it." Then, all of a sudden, Tom Reynolds decides he's not going to run so this rich Buffalo guy comes in and basically John was kicked aside 'cause this guy could self-finance and other stuff....except, they didn't know how tough this kid, Powers, is...he's still in it. I don't know how he's doing, but I still get e-mails all the time.

> ..."I can do more keeping these people on a moral plane than I can in a political office..."

Anyway it was more of a celebration at Tim's Washington service. The stories we told were good stories. Again, most of us were in shock. It was just that we couldn't believe Tim was gone. In the weeks that followed, I have probably more than one hundred e-mails from people. I sent out my recollections of the day and got a lot of e-mails back. I found out that there have been cancers, heart problems, and other diseases—and, at fifty-eight years old, I had been given a book by one of Tim and my classmates, Craig Roach, who runs Boston Consulting, a company here in D.C.. He's one of the smartest guys around. Craig told me about this book called *Younger Next Year*. It's written by a gerontologist and his seventy-year-old patient. It's written to guys in their fifties, telling how to prepare yourself for a later life. I'm correspondent for our alumni magazine and had put that in a column advising them to read this book. It tells all about what happens in your body when you exercise and when you don't. I spent two hundred words telling people about this book, and I got letters back saying, "Yeah, I've read this book and started to do it. I feel so much better."

"Tim brought us together."

Then Timmy dies. I'm hearing from all these guys my age who are facing mortality, who have had bouts with cancer and other things. Every time I think about passing on the treadmill or passing on lifting weights twice a week, I say, "Huh-uh," and I go downstairs.

There at the reception up on the rooftop, the time with the others was spent talking about where our years have gone. This was not in a maudlin way. We talked about how quickly they had gone by and about what we had done and what other guys were doing. It was a celebration in that we were all together again. Tim brought us together. Everyone said the same thing, "It's great to see you again. It's too bad the circumstances were so ------."

THESE SEVEN THINGS ARE TEN REASONS TO BE HOOKED ON RUSSERT

Bob Longo

Pittsburgh native and long-time California resident Bob Longo has been the most successful business grad of Tim Russert's friends. He was instrumental in helping Steve Jobs and Steve Wozniak build Apple into prominence in the early '80s.

At the time of Tim's wake, there was a group discussion that was being driven by Ben Bradlee and Dan Rather. There were a whole bunch of journalist types sitting around having a great discussion. Ben Bradlee said to all those guys, "We're all pretty famous people in the world of journalism. Who, at this table, thinks we're going to get this kind of a sendoff?" There's something different about this guy. It wasn't just that he was a famous journalist. When you look at that, even in terms of world figures or ex-presidents, I don't remember many other folks except for maybe Diana and Elvis who got that kind of attention.

The only other journalist who might get this kind of constant attention from multiple places might be Cronkite and I'm not even sure he would. It wasn't just NBC, it was across the board. Every media outlet showed it and the reaction came from all sectors and all across the political spectrum.

I was going into a meeting at Apple, and my son called me from Southern California. He thought I already knew. He said, "I really feel bad about Tim." I said, "What are you talking about?" He said, "Didn't you know Tim Russert died?" I was stunned. A bunch of us John Carroll guys got together in San Francisco to tip a few beers in Tim's honor. One guy, Marty Lindstrom, said he was sitting in a bar restaurant having a meal, and the TV was on.

He saw Russert's picture flashing. He told the group there that he and Tim were friends in college. One guy overheard him talking about Tim and came over and said, "Did you say you and Russert were friends?" He said, "Yes." "Do you know why he was just on the television?" The man told him, "He just died." Marty said he about fell off his chair. He just couldn't believe it. That was pretty much everybody's reaction. It was almost incredulous. It was even more so for those of us who knew Tim personally.

The John Carroll network is so strong, and we all use it all the time. For me, 'cause I've moved a lot, every town I've gone to, I get connected with a Carroll crowd. I've had people say to me, "How big was John Carroll?" It's small...two to three thousand kids. They'll say, "It sounds like everybody went to John Carroll." I think it's because everybody stays in touch. There are people you haven't seen for ten, fifteen years, and when you reconnect with them, it's like yesterday. They'll do you huge favors even though you haven't talked to them for ten years.

> They'll say, "It sounds like everybody went to John Carroll."

Freshman year, I got to know Tim because we were both campus politicos. At that time, we were on what they called the Dormitory Council. It was interesting because when we started at Carroll in '68, it was still a predominately all-male institution. We even still had to wear coats and ties to dinner at the beginning of our freshman year. It was just at the beginning of all the changes that really started to sweep the country. Carroll was still fairly conservative. If you know people in the Jesuit community, Carroll has always been on the conservative end, which is almost an oxymoron in Jesuit-speak that there would be anything conservative.

Tim and I saw ourselves as change agents. We were always involved in a lot of these crazy proposals, one of which was to change the dress code. We were putting bills in front of committees that were mostly made up of asking the Jesuits to let the students dress according to their lifestyles instead of wearing a coat and tie. We'd get into loggerheads with the Jezzies on that stuff.

When the first coeds started, we had a bill which was to have twenty-four-hour open dorms. Of course, most of the first women who boarded there at the university were alumni daughters. Not only were we fighting the Jesuits, we were fighting the alumni. Our compromise on twenty-four-hour open dorms was every other Sunday from two to four in the afternoon. Tim and I got accused of being sellouts.

With time, you would absolutely have done exactly the same thing. Of course, some of the old Jesuits were pretty outspoken. I remember one priest who was the ex-president of the University of Detroit, Father Maloren, who was on the committee when we were trying to change the dress code. We went to vote, and it was a 50-50 tie. One of the faculty people there was from the ed psych department, and he had all this data on why you should be dressed up and all this crazy stuff. Yet, when we voted, he abstained. Maloren was beating the heck out of this guy, calling him a coward because he didn't vote against the bill. I challenged Maloren and said, "You're didn't give us any reasons for your 'no' vote. Why don't you tell us why you think we shouldn't dress according to our lifestyle?" He said, "Do you really want to know?" I kept pressing and said, "Yeah, I really want to know." He said, "I don't want Dagos like you wearing Guinea shirts in the cafeteria." I turned to Tim and said, "I think I pushed him a little too far."

> "Tim and I saw ourselves as change agents.... always involved in a lot of these crazy proposals..."

When the first women came, one woman...and this woman ended up being the maid of honor at our wedding...was sitting in the front row on the first day of class. One of the priests came up to her and said, "Young lady, I took a vow of obedience, and I have to do what my superiors tell me, but while you're in my class, you'll close the gates of Hell." He made her cross her legs.

Now you look back on some of the early stuff and it sounds pretty comical.

Tim and I worked on Carl Stokes' campaign. He was the first black mayor of a major American city. A lot of the Kennedy operatives were a part of that. Cesar Chavez came in, and was here on election night. That was also the election when Tim and I worked on John Gilligan's campaign when he got elected governor of Ohio. His daughter is the governor of Kansas now. We were active in some of the external politics, as well as the internal politics.

Tim was the darling of the political science department. I started out Poly Sci and then switched to Communications somewhere along the way. Sheldon Gawiser, who became the chairman of the department at John Carroll and then moved on to become the chairman at Case Western Reserve was one of our professors. For the last thirty years or so, he has been a senior analyst at NBC.

> "Russert and I didn't know Cleveland from the man in the moon..."

He heads up all their polling. Shellie was one of the first people in the country who was doing computer projections. He was doing it for NBC, which was probably Tim's first connection to them. Then, Shellie probably ended up working for Tim all these years.

When we worked on those early political campaigns, it was all a lot of fun. A few months ago, I got invited to a function back in Pittsburgh where Tim was speaking. I couldn't make it. A guy who is pretty well known from John Carroll, Howard "Hoddy" Hanna, who was head of Young Democrats, was from Pittsburgh and Central Catholic and was the one who got me involved in some of those activities. Anyway, years before we all got put on a bus to go canvass houses for Stokes. Russert and I didn't know Cleveland from the man in the moon at that time so they put us in a van. They took us around town and we ended up discovering one of the worst ghettos. It had some of the worst riots. We were met by Black Panthers who had Doberman pinscher dogs with them and they were taking us around while we were knocking on doors there.

The black people we came across were extremely friendly and supportive. You'd hit these ethnic pockets of white folks who still lived in some of those areas and they were more angry at these "white suburban kids" going in and knocking on the doors for the black candidate.

> "Everybody else there knew that Russert was tricking Duffy with these empty cans."

There were seven or eight of us living together in a house. One of these guys, Joe Duffy from Chicago, worshipped Tim. Maybe he was a lot more perceptive than the rest of us were back then about Tim's potential greatness. Tim had a great sense of humor and realized how gullible Joe was. Tim would use a can opener to empty out a couple of the beer cans from the bottom. Then, he'd challenge Duff to a drinking contest. He'd pop the tab off the can and throw it off in a second and quickly slam it down. Then he'd have Duffy lift the can. Duffy would lift the empty can and would just shake his head, "Tim, how can anybody drink like that?" He would be wide-eyed—absolutely amazed that Russert could drink these beers straight down so quickly. Everybody else there knew that Russert was tricking Duffy with these empty cans. Duffy always saw Tim as the next Bobby Kennedy—saw him as bigger than life. He was probably more perceptive, even though we thought he was more gullible at the time. Duff was a great guy.

Pretty early on I remember politicos were trying to get Russert to take the congressional seat in western New York around Buffalo, which I think would have been pretty easy for him to do. This was after he helped Moynihan bring in western New York. One time, I actually asked Tim why he didn't run for a political office. He said that it was a lot more fun for him behind the scenes. He really enjoyed that. The other part, and what probably drew him to journalism, was the fact that you have to make a lot of compromises when you're in the front...and even when you're in the back. When you start to get into the journalism side, particularly the way he did it, then you can go search for truth. For a lot of people, that's a lot happier place to be—to seek the truth rather than having to compromise and often have to do things you don't believe in. This was a lot closer to his own personal values and his own internal feelings about the world and about what made him happy. Minimum, we always expected that Russert could have easily been the Press Secretary or some other kind of position even if he didn't go for an elected office. He really stayed on his course. He ended up coming to everybody's attention and shining. He was the very rare person who was always seeking the truth.

When we were at Carroll, I had been class president for three years. Then going into our senior year, Tim and I and a couple of other guys were very active on campus. We had this meeting about what we were doing for our senior year. Tim said, "Bob, I think you ought to run for the union president". I said, "I don't have the time or desire to run for class president again. Tim, this is really your destiny to be the union president." Everybody else agreed. I always remember him in effect somewhat respectfully offering it to me. He was definitely the savior campus politician as well as this good human. Then we lined up all the different characters to nominate and second him. One of the guys who called me after Tim died had been a football player at Carroll. I had forgotten that I had gotten this guy to do one of the seconds for Russert when he was running for union president 'cause he wanted to show that one of the jocks would stand up and nominate him. We had people from the underground groups, guys from the military industrial complex, the ROTC Pershing Rifles. We had this guy from the football team. We had all walks of life seconding the nomination.

> "He was the very rare person who was always seeking the truth."

I look back on it, and we were all full of ourselves. But, it was a pretty interesting time just because of the social doings. Tim was really good at being involved in all those spheres. He was very involved in some of the campus activities that were going on with the Vietnam War and with the changes that were going on nationally on college campuses. He was conscious of all that. The highest honor, when you're a senior at John Carroll, is the coveted Senior Award, which isn't really a popularity thing. It's more who represents the values of the university, and particularly the Jesuits. Tim, hands down, got that honor when we graduated.

A few years later, I went back to John Carroll and was on the faculty. That was really a lot of fun for me. One of my ex-professors was a young Jesuit, Paul Shervish, who had taught my sociology classes. He ended up leaving Carroll to become chief of staff for Father Robert Drinan who was the Jesuit who went to Congress. When I was on the faculty, Father Paul came back for a visit. Paul came in to the Rathskeller, saw me and came over and sat down. He said, "Haven't you graduated yet?" I said, "I hate to tell you, Father, I'm on the faculty." He said, "Oh my God, the proletariat has taken over."

> "...I would have had him on YouTube and the whole country would have seen Tim Russert singing in the john."

One thing happened, unfortunately, before cell phones had cameras on them. We were all staying in one of the dorms at Carroll at one of our reunions. I went in the common bathroom to shave one morning and I heard somebody singing at the top of his lungs in one of the stalls. It was Russert. I didn't know whether he was still feeling good from the night before, but I was thinking that today I would have had him on YouTube and the whole country would have seen Tim Russert singing in the john. I don't remember what he was singing, but I do remember that he was having a good time.

A group of us—with Russert as the ringleader—were making the rounds. We went to the Indianapolis 500, the Kentucky Derby, maybe Mardi Gras. We went to Notre Dame when Johnny Cash was singing there. Russert loved Notre Dame. The campus is incredibly beautiful. You get some of these guys from southern Indiana and southern Ohio and places like that, they were big country-western fans. They got some of the rest of us involved.

One of the interesting things for me was I-Chi, which was the rival fraternity to the U-Club, which was Russert's fraternity. A lot of the campus political people and also the sports captains were either U-Clubbers or I-Chis so you were in one group or the other. When I first started in I-Chis, they were the more "men about campus" so they weren't insular. Then the fraternities started to get a little more inward bound. I was getting more involved in external campus and outside-the-campus activities. I became good friends with a lot of the U-Clubbers. I started to go to more of the U-Club parties and U-Club activities with Tim and a lot of those guys.

A few years ago, I had a company I spun out of Carnegie Mellon. I had raised about twenty million dollars in investments. My lead investors were a group out of Florida. The head guy in this was a kind of bean counter, by background. I think he didn't believe half of the stuff we often were talking about. One time

"It was…a reaction where this guy didn't believe that I really knew Russert…"

at a board meeting, the discussion was who do we know in the big-boy media that we might be able to leverage to see if we can't get some attention. I mentioned in passing that I was friends with Tim Russert. It was almost like a reaction where this guy didn't believe that I really knew Russert…like it was some kind of bravado on my part, or something like that. Nothing really came of that. A few months later at another board meeting, this guy comes in and goes, "By the way, I met your buddy, Russert." I already knew it 'cause Tim had called me after he met this guy. He met him at a fundraiser on Nantucket. Tim said the guy came up to him and acted like he didn't believe that I knew him. Tim said this guy was backing into the conversation. He said, "We might, sorta, kinda, have a mutual friend." Once Tim realized this guy was feeling him out to see if I really knew him, Tim started to really play up the relationship. In fact, this guy later told me, "He kept calling you Bobby Longo." I said, "Well, he always did call me Bobby." I took it as affectionate because of Bobby Kennedy. So Tim did this thing with him, where he gave him some kind of code thing. He said, "Tim wanted me to tell you this. I don't know what it means. He said you'll know what it means." I didn't know what it meant either, but it seemed to this guy that Tim and I had this kind of code language that was going back and forth. He said something to me, and I answered back, "Oh yeah, yeah."

> "Once Tim realized this guy was feeling him out to see if I really knew him, Tim started to really play up the relationship."

Recently, I bumped into Tim at Dulles. We were coming in from different flights. We were at the baggage claim getting our bags. It was funny because I remember there was a billboard there with his picture on it. We chatted a while. He offered me a ride in his limo, but I already had a ride. I was supposed to go back a few months ago when he was at this thing in Pittsburgh that Hoddy Hanna was doing—some sort of a charity fundraiser. Tim had agreed to come in and speak. There was a whole bunch of us who were part of the Pittsburgh John Carroll crowd. It was interesting because afterward I had two or three different guys call me and say, "Tim was asking about you and was wondering whether or not you were going to be here." It was one of those things where I tried to see if I could work out my schedule, and I couldn't. Now I regret it because it would have been my last time to really have had a chance to see Tim.

I've noticed other people like Tim who grew up successful. They grew up in that middle class ethnic Catholic culture. It was a value kind of thing they learned. It taught them not only the religious and spiritual values, but the work ethic, the importance of education. There was a lot of that. World War II. The Depression. Parents really saw the American ideal and had those kinds of hopes for the next generation. Tim embodied all of that. All of us got a piece of it. We probably didn't put it all together. It seems like all of those different kinds of virtues and values that got espoused that were part of the American ideal, part of the Christian or Catholic ideals—he really believed those things at the core. Most of the folks I know like that—they weren't fuddy-duddies. They were people who hung out in church all the time. There was a balance there. They knew how to have fun. They knew how to give back and contribute.

> "There was a balance there. They knew how to have fun...."

On TV, you'd see Tim browbeat these guests sometimes. Take Condoleezza Rice or John McCain. Then he'd be asking them about their favorite football team or who was playing the Bills that weekend. There'd be this friendly chit-chat that would go on. The sports analogy is probably the good one. The professional athlete can be out there on the field mano-a-mano with some teammate from college or a good friend or even a brother. After the game, they will go out to dinner with them. During the game, they'll go beat each other's brains out. The other piece with Tim is he became a person whose career was truth seeking. He could do it. He naturally enjoyed it and it felt right to him. The journalism side really became that for him.

I didn't get to know his wife, Maureen. I knew of her. I would hear different things once I came out here. She was from the Berkeley area. Occasionally, I would get word—there were a couple of times when guys were getting together with Tim and I would be out of town. I only heard great things about Maureen and, of course, Luke. I always laughed about Luke because there was an older guy in Tim's fraternity who I knew pretty well, Luke McNoto. I always knew that Tim thought highly of Luke so when I heard stories about how Luke got his name, I always thought about Luke McNoto as somebody Tim had a high regard for and may have named his son after.

"I only heard great things about Maureen and, of course, Luke."

Tim was so adept at relationship management. There was a situation one time. I was complaining to him about how apathetic our class was. It wasn't apathetic in the larger social sense—actually very active in that sense—but in doing some of the more tactical things that need to be done in terms of the class management. I was having a hard time finding a class editor for our news stories for the school newspaper. We were in the snack bar at John Carroll. Tim sees this kid sitting in the back by himself. I don't remember the kid's name, but Tim went up to him and asked him if he was in our class. He said he was. Tim asked what his major was. I think it was English. Tim said, "How would you like to be the class news editor?" This guy was looking around like, "You mean me?" Tim said, "Yeah." This guy said, "Yeah." This was probably a student nobody ever talked to. I used to call them "rock" people. You'd pick up a rock—they were there. They generally were commuter students and didn't really have many relationships on campus.

Tim had this ability to not only make them feel important and part of things, but to enable that kind of support. Those kind of people would die for him. He picked them out of obscurity and, all of a sudden, they became someone. All the rest of us would end up with these work burdens where we were doing it all ourselves. Tim always had this entourage of people who were doing things for him because he was so good at the relationship management part of it. He was masterful. He looked at it and saw how he was able to bring forces together to solve a problem or getting involved in some kind of a rally or some kind of a protest thing. One of my father-in-laws' friends had made a comment like that to me: "I heard you're a friend of that Russert guy." We were in college and they saw us as these rabble-rousers...and we were, to some extent. I think the faculty valued that.

Russert had to check what was going on, both at a macro level and a micro level. When I first heard Tim was going to be on television, I wasn't surprised to see his rise at NBC. Having been on the corporate side, I understand how companies are just as political as political organizations are. So you have to learn how to deal with those relationships as well. When you have the management skills Tim had, I knew he'd be successful there. I was not surprised when he was moving up the ladder at NBC and had the *Today Show* and a lot of those other things reporting in to him. Then, all of a sudden, he shifted to becoming the Washington bureau chief. He took the *Meet the Press* job and got more focused on the news and being the political expert and left the "climbing the ladder" at NBC. Tim was the kind of person who could probably have been running NBC or GE someday if that's what he wanted. Again, he had those kind of skills.

> "He picked them out of obscurity and, all of a sudden, they became someone."

Tim, like a lot of the guys who came out of the Jesuit high schools, had an easier time at a place like Carroll. They came in much more prepared. There's also a certain halo you got when you're able to be successful from the get-go when you come into a place like Carroll. From that standpoint, I think it was easier. He and I were in a political television course with Professor Sheldon Gawiser. I didn't see Tim work very hard in that course 'cause he really didn't have to. In the courses that were more rigorous, Tim still had a high grade point. He was the president of Alpha Sigma Nu, which was the Jesuit honors fraternity. You don't get there by screwing off in all your classes. Tim was able to use his intelligence and skills, but in some cases, I think he got a pass.

Doug Webber was a great guy. He was from Jasper, Indiana, way down south. Jasper was one of the teams that played in the *Hoosiers* movie. Webb's brother was All-State in basketball, and his dad was the editor of *Hoopla* magazine. He would call the home operator to get the basketball scores. He went to Brebeuf in Indianapolis, and that was a long way from Jasper. Webb graduated from Carroll either summa or magna cum laude. On purpose, he took every hard course with every professor who had a rigorous reputation. He seemed like a hick, right? At graduation, when his achievements were announced, there was almost this gasp. Most people didn't realize. I remember the night before the exams, which was one hundred multiple choice questions, he finally cracked the book and surveyed it...and got one hundred out of one hundred on it. Russert was aghast.

> "By and large, the kids who came out of the Jesuit schools were much better prepared."

Some of these guys—certainly they went in there with native intelligence—were able to navigate in that Jesuit environment. I came out of a Christian Brothers high school, and we had to spend our freshman and sophomore years getting ourselves up to that speed. It was a lot more challenging at Carroll. By and large, the kids who came out of the Jesuit schools were much better prepared. I saw that overall. Tim was a good example of that, as well. That's why you hear that reverence that is held for the Jesuits, and particularly the guys out of the high schools. It's more than a mystique.

I was hosting a dinner. It was CIOs from a lot of prestigious and top universities, and so I had most of the Ivy League CIOs at this dinner. I had executives from Stanford and Carnegie Mellon and University of Chicago. One of the questions I asked them was, "If you had your education to do all over, where would you go to undergrad?" Almost every single person said they would go to a smaller college. They said they could always specialize in graduate school. You never get that kind of broad based liberal arts underpinning they all felt was really valuable. On top of it, in most of those smaller schools, you also get a rich social education. You get to know the people you are going to school with. You have more personal connections with the faculty. There's more mentoring that goes on. All those things most of us discovered at a place like Carroll.

Of course Tim's death makes you examine your own mortality. I went through a battle with cancer about two years ago. It was pretty clear we were getting ready to sell the company again. I was going through a normal executive physical at Stanford. I had no symptoms and felt I was in pretty good shape, had a trainer and a nutritionist and

> "...in most of those smaller schools, you also get a rich social education."

had been working out. The last test they did was the colonoscopy. The gastroenterologist, as she was doing the test, was saying, "The good news is that you won't have to have this for another ten years." Then there was this "oops." They found a pretty good sized tumor on the cusp of my colon and rectum. Steve Jobs had just gone through treatment for cancer so I called him and he got me set up with his oncologist and some of his doctor teams. I went through chemo and radiation and all that. I've been clear now for almost two years. Fortunately it hadn't metastasized or spread, which was just dumb luck because it could have been going on for as much as eight to ten years.

I now look at the fact that I had a disease that could be treated and sometimes cured...so, you don't think of yourself as lucky when getting cancer...but, in my family, there was an awful lot of cancer and early heart disease. My dad died young. His brother was forty-nine and dropped dead at a Super Bowl party. So, it's that sense that you don't get a second chance.

I have another very good friend and neighbor in Pittsburgh who had worked for IBM had a very similar thing to Tim. He literally sat up in bed one morning and fell back down, and that was it. In his case, there weren't a whole lot of early signs that there was something wrong. You see those kinds of things, and it does bring focus on your own mortality.

One of my younger brothers, after a friend's parent had passed away said, "You do realize we're becoming the old people." You see people a lot younger than you retiring.

I'm so glad I went to John Carroll. I'd go back there in a flash. It's one of those things where if you had it to do all over, it would be really hard not to do it again. There's more prestige at the schools like Harvard or Notre Dame, but you don't get that very tight and personal thing that I got out of Carroll. I think that's part of what you're trading off.

"...it does bring focus on your own mortality."

At John Carroll, we had ice-breaker mixers for all the girls at the Catholic high schools. They had that freshman dance, and I met my wife my first week at Carroll. We got married on Memorial Day, the day after graduation. My dad was in the food business so my brothers and I all got married on a holiday so he wouldn't have to close the store on a Saturday. One brother was married on Thanksgiving and another on Labor Day. We used to tease my dad and say, "Dad, when you die, we're going to have to lay you out in the meat case so we don't have to close the store."

18   Bonn
25   Rio B

MAY   2   The B

KULAS AUDITO

Tim Russert was president of the Student Union at John Carroll University in
University Heights, Ohio. He graduated in 1972 with a BA in Political Science.

After graduating from John Carroll, Russert went on to earn his law degree from Cleveland-Marshall School of Law in Cleveland, Ohio, in 1976.

Tim Russert shows excitement during the Duke-Boston College NCAA basketball game in Boston, Wednesday, February 1, 2006. The second-ranked Blue Devils hung on to defeat BC 83-81.

On cake: #1 Streak Continues 5 Years and Counting

On magazine: The #1 Sunday morning program 5 years in a row.

Tim Russert speaks to guests as *Meet the Press* celebrates its first place in ratings among Sunday talk shows, five years in a row, April 30, 2006 at the NBC studios in Washington.

Russert was a key prosecution witness in the Lewis "Scooter" Libby CIA leak trial in February, 2007.

MSNBC debate moderator Tim Russert speaks to the audience before a debate of Democratic presidential hopefuls at Dartmouth College September, 26, 2007 in Hanover, NH.

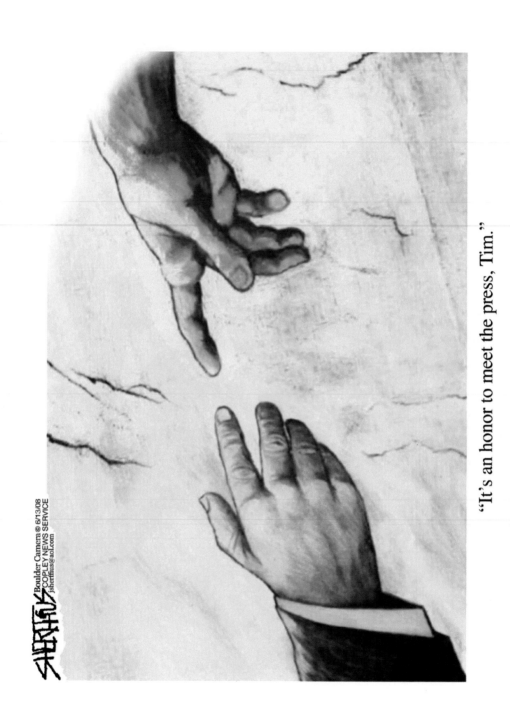

"It's an honor to meet the press, Tim."

A flag and NBC logo are visible at the childhood home of Tim Russert on Flag Day, June 14, 2008 in Buffalo, New York.

New York Governor-elect Mario Cuomo, right, joins Timothy Russert, 32, in New York, Dec. 9, 1982 following the formal announcement that Russert has been selected to direct Cuomo's news media operations.

Three generations of the Russert family pose for a portrait with manager Joe Torre, of the New York Yankees, prior to a game in 2006.

Washington: First in War, First in Peace, Last in the National League. Russert at a Washington Nationals game in '05.

Tim Russert with his son Luke and the NHL Stanley Cup June 7, 1998 in Washington, DC. The Washington Capitals hockey team was in the Stanley Cup finals for the first time in the team's history.

Now, let's meet your Buffalo Bisons: from left, Luke Russert, Tim "Big Russ" Russert, and T.J.—Tim Russert.

PRESIDENT TO THE WELL, AND THERE WOULD B.. A DEBATE OVER WHETHER

A technician in a cherry picker works on the giant video screen in New York's Times Square, September 21, 1998, as NBC's Tim Russert comments on President Clinton's videotaped grand jury testimony from August 17, 1998.

Homicide: Life on the Street—"The Old and the Dead" Episode 16—aired March 3, 1995. Pictured: (left to right) Tim Russert as Himself, Isabella Hofmann as Lt./Capt. Megan Russert, Daniel Baldwin as Det. Beau Felton. The fictional character Megan Russert was his "cousin." The show was created by a fellow Buffalo Canisius Prep grad.

Tim Russert Bobblehead Day, June 4,
2005 at Buffalo's Dunn Tire Park.

Russert with Pamela Anderson on the *Tonight Show* with Jay Leno on April 12, 2005.

Russert fans pay homage at a makeshift memorial at the base of a wooden sculpture of Tim Russert in Buffalo, NY, Monday, June 16, 2008.

A long way from South Buffalo, Russert flanked by Chris Wallace, the President and Katie Couric shortly before his passing.

The City of Buffalo honors one of their own.

Emmett O'Neill, left, plays basketball with Matt Eagen, right, in Tim Russert's Children's Garden in Buffalo, NY, Friday, June 13, 2008—the day of Russert's passing.

Tim Russert's Children's Garden

— EST. 2002 —

South Buffalo Alive

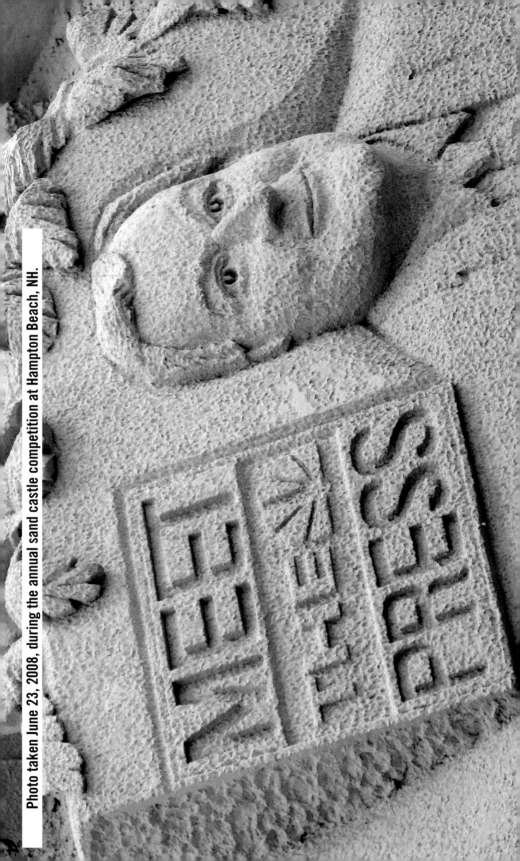

Democratic strategist James Carville and his wife, Republican strategist Mary Matalin burst into tears during a taping of *Meet the Press* June 15, 2008.

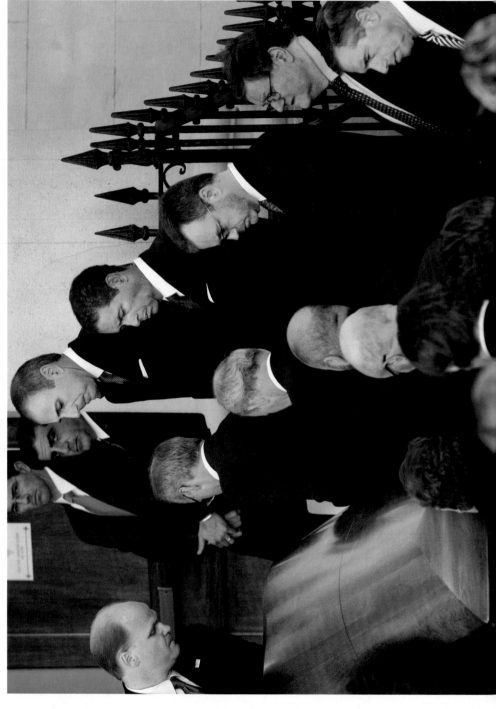

The casket of Tim Russert is carried into Holy Trinity Church in the Georgetown area of Washington, June 18, 2008. At top right are, NBC *Today Show* host Matt Lauer and Bryant Gumbel of *HBO Sports*.

The Blue Streaks ride again. Gathering after Tim Russert's service are his closest friends from his college days at John Carroll University. What appears to be gray hair might actually be ultra-blonde. Not visible is a double rainbow that formed in the background.

Tim Russert and wife, Maureen Orth.

Items placed at a makeshift memorial at Tim Russert Park in West Seneca, NY, June 16, 2008.

If it's Sunday Morning....
it will never be the
same....
Meet The Press.
GO TIM!!
♡ South Buffalo

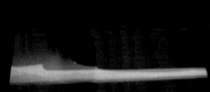

Luke Russert touches the empty chair that
was left behind by his father on the set of
Meet the Press after a taping June 15, 2008
at the NBC studios in Washington, DC.

A COACH IS A TEACHER WITH A DEATH WISH

Tom Narducci

Tom Narducci was a standout football player at Central Catholic High School in Pittsburgh—Dan Marino's alma mater—and continued his stellar play at John Carroll. Narducci is now a successful high school football coach at Hudson (Ohio) High School.

Tim was in a fraternity called the University Club, and I was in I-Chi. We had a lot of common friends and were very competitive with one another. There were no national fraternities at John Carroll at that time; everything was local.

The best way I could describe Tim is we're at our twenty-fifth reunion. Tim was at the reunion. I go, "Isn't it amazing? Russert is a national figure in this country and when you think about him back at John Carroll, he was one of the guys running around the dorm late at night looking for food like the rest of us."

Our senior year, Tim was running for student union president. Bob Longo and I were best friends, and we grew up right down the street from one another in Pittsburgh. We both went to Central Catholic together and then made our way to John Carroll. Bob Longo was going to run for class president, and Tim Russert was going to run for student body president. Longo was going to be Russert's campaign manager. He and Russert came to me and said, "Hey, Duch, how about giving a seconding speech for Tim at the meeting for his nomination for president of the student union?" I felt pretty good—"Hey, these guys are realizing my political value here on this campus." Well, no sooner was that said than Longo said, "Hey, wear your football letter jacket when you give the speech." A little while later, Russert said, "Now Duch, make sure you wear your football letter jacket and everyone can see that it's a football letter jacket...." As I kidded around with those guys, I go "Yeah. I'm the token jock." I'm endorsing liberal Tim Russert for the student union presidency.

> "Russert is a national figure...he was one of the guys running around the dorm late at night looking for food like the rest of us."

I don't even remember what I said in the speech, but it would have been a five to ten minute speech. Of course, I had my letter jacket on. My hair was down over my ears. It was the off-season. Tim was our student union president...and I was glad to endorse him. Tim was a good guy in college. He was just one of the guys. He played rugby. He drank beer with us. I'm sure Tim would have come to our football games. If he didn't, he was partying with us after the games.

Our college years were 1968 to 1972, and 3.2 beer was allowed in Ohio. We actually had a bar on campus. We had the Rathskeller. It was right below, of all places to build it, the chapel. That place would go strong every day, except on Saturday night at five o'clock, when it had to shut down because they had Mass upstairs in the chapel. There was a place called the Pepper Pot, down the road close to Murray Hill, that was real popular back then.

Between the I-Chis and the U-Club guys, we all would end up at the same parties and at the same gatherings. I don't remember that Tim had a girlfriend. He struck gold when he married Maureen because she was really something. I thought it was funny when I read some of the comments Luke made that Tim "married up," and he did. He did—he married up. He outkicked his coverage on that deal.

I'm one of those oddities—I'm a high school teacher, in education, and I'm a Republican, as is my wife. I'm the minority. I was born and raised a Democrat. Same thing—my dad, if he knew that I was a staunch Republican—no matter who ran, he was voting a straight Democratic ticket. The Democrats lost me with Bill Clinton. My wife, early on, would just get so mad because she said, "That Tim Russert, that friend of yours, he helped Clinton get elected. He's part of that liberal media." Then, when she had a chance to meet Tim at one of the reunions, she goes, "Tim is a pretty good guy." I go, "Yeah." My wife is an Irish Catholic as well. I said, "He's Irish Catholic, what more do you want? How bad can he be?"

When I read Russert's first book, I sat there and just said, "This is tremendous." Tim put into words what we all feel. We all have parents. My dad was a shoemaker. My dad owned a shoe repair shop in Pittsburgh right across from J&L Steel Mills. The big thing for him was for me to go to college and to go to graduate school. We were all those types of kids. Not everybody at John Carroll was the son of a doctor or a lawyer or a big-time businessperson. Our dads were immigrants and truck drivers and shoemakers and Longo's dad owned a grocery store and Russert's dad worked on a garbage truck. We all shared in that common background about just how important that college education was.

> "He's Irish Catholic, what more do you want? How bad can he be?"

I've kidded around with some of our classmates. I go, "You know. I'm glad the Sam's Clubs carried Tim's books so I didn't have to pay full price for a Tim Russert book." I'm glad Luke and Maureen get the royalties on them. Tim was so eloquent in that first book. And then the second, the letters—we all could have written a letter telling about our dads and the impact they had on our lives and how important that college education was. We all shared that when we were at John Carroll. So many of us kids were the first generation going to college with parents who were struggling.

There was not anyone who was jealous of Russert's success. We all *wore* the fact that we knew Tim Russert—it's like a badge of honor. I can't tell you how many times I would say, "Hey, I went to school with Tim Russert," or "Hey, I'm a classmate of Tim

Russert." I think we all just shared in his success. We have a class at school called New Dimensions. Every year, they spend a week in New York in the spring. Just before the attack on Iraq they had to cancel the trip because of the concern with terrorists. The two teachers and the one young girl, a John Carroll graduate, adored Tim Russert. Her Sunday mornings were scheduled around *Meet the Press*. She said, "Do you think Tim Russert would come in and do a debate with us?" I said, "I'll tell you what. I'll call him. The worst thing that could happen is that he would not be able to do it." I called, and I wasn't able to get to Tim. His secretary called me back the next day and said, "Tim said he would love to do it, but he can't leave because of the war. He's got to be here around the clock for coverage. But, if you ever want to do it at another time, please call. He'd love to come up and do it."

On June 13, I was on my way home. I have Sirius radio and was listening to FOX News. They interrupted the broadcast to make the announcement. Like everyone else, I was just stunned. It was, "Oh, I'm not hearing this. There has to be something that's not right about this." Then, I got home and turned on the TV. I saw the replay of Tom Brokaw making the announcement.... That wasn't supposed to happen. Tim should still be here and enjoying a great career and growing old with us—we should all grow old together. He should be enjoying his son and grandkids someday. It just shouldn't have happened.

> "That wasn't supposed to happen. Tim should still be here..."

With what's happened to Tim, I absolutely think about my own mortality. It shouldn't have happened, but we're all headed there. We just hope that we get to lead a longer, more prosperous life. I kid around with my mom, who is eighty-six. My dad passed away a few years ago. She's a little old Italian woman. "Why doesn't God take me? Why doesn't God take me? I should be with my husband." I always kid her, "Mom, God takes the good young."

So, Tim is up there with the best 'cause he was certainly taken. Tony Snow—the same thing. Those are names of quality people who died way too early. I know people who scheduled their Sunday church around *Meet the Press*. They wanted to watch it, and they wanted to hear Tim and wanted to see what he had to say and who he was going to interview that week. That's the way Tim was. That's what was so appealing about Tim is that he was very personable and everyone felt comfortable with him.

RUSSERT WENT OUT FOR BASKETBALL IN HIGH SCHOOL BUT THEY DIDN'T NEED ONE

David Carden

David Carden is the Director of Operations for the state of Illinois for Cold Stone Creamery ice cream stores. He lives in the western Chicago suburbs. He was Tim Russert's buddy in both high school and college.

I was on the Acrians basketball team with Tim when we were high school freshmen. We were a group of guys who were too short to play for the high school team. We would play at the halftime of the college games—Canisius College, St. Bonnie's, Niagara. The Acrians would play grade school teams. We'd run out there at half time and play for twenty minutes. Russert, who was a big guy—6'1" as an adult—but when we started that year he was only about 5'4". Tim was a very ambitious guy. He was as regular as anybody could be, but whereas the rest of us were just blindly running around trying to figure out what the h--- was going on, he had a plan...and he was working it.

When we get to John Carroll, everybody is feeling their way. But, Tim always had a plan he was working. He eventually became the student union president. We always used to make fun of him saying, "You can sell your bill of goods to all these people, but we know you from high school...!" He'd say, "Hey, keep this to yourself." This was way before someone coined the saying, "What happens in Vegas, stays in Vegas."

Tim was involved in everything at John Carroll. I roomed one semester with him. At the end of freshmen year, I was told I had a room for sophomore year on campus. I get a letter during the course of the summer saying, "We don't have a room for you." My father said, "We're pulling you out of there." I convinced him I wanted to stay, and we got a room with a retired couple who took in students. Russert was living with a friend of ours named Duke.

We were at a social gathering, a mixer, in between Thanksgiving and Christmas. Our friend Duke had a few cocktails—your typical *Animal House* type behavior. He goes to this mixer in a fog. The girls had left their purses laying on the bleachers, and Duke starts going through these purses. He gets caught by one of the security guys. Out comes the security cop, pulling Duke over to the side. In comes Russert who, at the time, is living with Duke.

Russert intervenes. He steps up and trying to calm the situation says, "I'm with the Dean of Student Affairs, and I'll take charge of this gentleman and bring him over to the Dean of Men." Russert is trying to get Duke out of it so they could run for the door. The cop starts to do it but says, "No. I'd better call the police on this one. I'll be right back." He's got Duke by the arm. He turns around...Russert is gone. Russert gave it his best shot and then he's

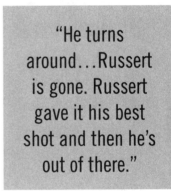

"He turns around...Russert is gone. Russert gave it his best shot and then he's out of there."

out of there. So...on-campus living is not for everybody! Now, good ole me, who has spent his six months off-campus is now back on campus...and I get to go to the recently-vacated Duke spot in Russert's room in Murphy Hall. Between the two of us, we were into so many different odds and ends, we very seldom spent any time in the room.

We knew people who lived off-campus, so on weekends we invaded them. We never wanted to stay in the dorm room over the weekend because of the curfews.

Senior year Russert was living off-campus, as we all did. I had a bet with the guy who ran the cafeteria. He came up to me and said, "Hey Dave, you're not supposed to be in the cafeteria. You don't have a pass. You live off-campus." I said, "But there are plenty of other people in here like that." He said, "Nobody, whatsoever, gets into this place." Russert and I always had this big rivalry because he was the president of University Club at the time I was involved with the I-Chis. He said, "Can you give me an example?" I said, "What about Russert?" He goes, "He never gets in the building." I said, "How about this, Ed? The next time I point Russert out to you in this place, you owe me a case of wine." Here I am, twenty years old, and I'm not supposed to be doing this. He goes, "Yeah, that's fine." About two weeks later, I come through the back door, *with Russert*. I felt real good about what I knew was about to happen. Russert went over to sit with the other University Club group, and I would go over to the group I was with, either the rugby team or the I-Chis. Ed comes in through the front door and sees me. He walks up and says, "Dave, what's up?" I said, "I don't know. I just walked in with that guy over there sitting at the table." He looks over at the table and sees Russert. Sure enough...that night, Ed shows up and says, "Here's the keys to the place. Come on. I've got a couple of bottles of wine. I'm not giving you a case of wine." I show up with Jace Caulfield and a couple of other friends. This guy has a little ice chest with about six bottles of wine in it. When I say "wine" and you think "wine" we're not talking the same thing...if you follow my drift! This guy runs the cafeteria, and he wants to go home at about eleven o'clock. We've still got a couple of bottles to drink. We say, "Just leave the keys. I'll lock up for you. I'll give them to you tomorrow when I come back." He gave me the keys and never once said another word to me when Russert or I would come in to eat for free. It was too ambitious of a plan to think you were going to prevent Russert from getting in.

> "When we were at John Carroll, I believe Russert literally had the keys to every building."

When we were at John Carroll, I believe Russert literally had the keys to every building. I don't think I'm exaggerating there. He was the type of guy who was involved in everything...on both sides of the fence. By that, I mean he was the student council president. He was involved in a lot of the debates at the time—national issues—the real issues going on. But, he was also on the flip side, involved in every shenanigan, whether it was getting into the cafeteria, getting into the Rathskeller, getting into this or that free. He crossed that fence very well. And always did.

At our place they had this woman, Shirley, who was on the cafeteria front door, and you didn't get by Shirley without a meal ticket or close inspection, unless you really went to great lengths, which some people mastered after a while. Russert schmoozed Shirley, "Beautiful. Shirley, you look wonderful." "Oh, Tim," and he'd be by the door. Or, he'd be coming in the back door 'cause he had the key to the place....

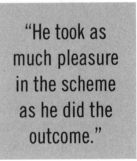

"He took as much pleasure in the scheme as he did the outcome."

I wouldn't say Tim was a good basketball player, but he was competitive. He was always very competitive at anything, whether it was high school or college. We'd do the intramurals, and he played for the University Club's football team. He was like a wild man. Tim was not long on talent, and I don't want to knock his athletic ability, but much longer on heart. He was very, very competitive and that was everywhere—athletics or academics. Tim was trying to build a résumé when he was twelve. So what if he couldn't spell it or thought it was a French word....

Tim was always looking out for others, but he was always a schemer. He took as much pleasure in the scheme as he did the outcome. When he was at John Carroll, we would give him a hard time and say, "You've got a lot of these characters fooled, they think you're the class act and the student council president...but we know the real deal." He goes, "Heeeey! We don't need to be discussing these details." We'd say, "One for the students—one for T.J." But we weren't allowed to say that outside of our immediate circle. We didn't want to damage his reputation.

The last time I saw Tim was two years ago when he did the second book. He comes to Chicago for the book tour. I didn't get to do the one in Chicago, but then he did one in Naperville, over at Pfeiffer Hall, which is part of North Central College. I go there to see him. He had been driven from downtown. He's jumping out of this car, and I bump into him out in front of this place. He's got the official college student guide with him, and I'm going, "Hey, T.J., you want to stop over here." He looks up and comes running over and we're talking. This kid with him is trying to figure out what's going on because I'm throwing verbal jabs at him and giving him a hard time. This kid is looking at me like I'm molesting or accosting him. We get in there. Now, this is typical Russert. He comes out on the stage and goes, "Hey, I want to throw a shout out to an old friend of mine from Canisius High School and John Carroll days. Dave, get up on your feet." Well, I'm not getting up on my feet, but that was the type guy he was. He'd reached the pinnacle of success, but he never forget who he was or where he was from. He was the most loyal guy going. He was always looking to try to help somebody else out or do anything he could to try to make life better for someone else. I saw him last fall at South Bend when Boston College was there playing football. Once Luke started going to B.C., Russert came in every other year for the Notre Dame–B.C. game.

> "Tim was the most normal guy in the world... but he lived in two different worlds."

Tim was the most normal guy in the world...but he lived in two different worlds. When he had official functions, he was always watching his Ps and Qs. But get him at a John Carroll reunion, where he could sit back where everybody knew him as Tim or T.J., he would let the guard down when he wasn't around people who were looking at his public persona.

IF YOU'RE LUCKY ENOUGH TO HAVE TIM RUSSERT AS YOUR BEST FRIEND, YOU'RE LUCKY ENOUGH

Marty Bergerson

Marty Bergerson and Tim Russert could have been twins...except Russert had his Buffalo Bills and Boston College while Bergerson had his Chicago Cubs and Notre Dame. They were best friends for forty years. Among his other ventures, Bergerson runs Bergy's Sports Bar, the place to be in his hometown of Michigan City, Indiana.

I play a lot of golf at Long Beach Country Club. We have about seven members who are John Carroll guys. The pros and others call us the "John Carroll mafia." "It's like you guys are all hooked at the hip with each other." I've got a really good friend who graduated from Loyola University in '72. He goes, "You guys are unbelievable. I hardly see anybody I graduated with. That's all you guys do."

In September of '68, I went to school. Tim Russert was in the same dorm, and we were both political science majors. We both were white, Irish-Catholic knuckleheads who liked to drink. We joined the same fraternity. I had a lot of classes with Tim. We ran together, same fraternity. He roomed with me for a while. We got along like a couple of knuckleheads.

Tim was extremely loyal. I knew he was bright; I just didn't know he was going to be so successful. I talked to him the Friday before he died. I probably was the last friend he was BS-ing with. He was out to dinner with his wife and another couple. We were talking and I asked him what he was up to. He said he was doing his show on Sunday and then he and Maureen were flying to Italy and "we're going to see Luke, and then I've got to get back on Thursday for the show. I'm probably going to come in for a Cubs game. Now that the primaries are over, I can relax a little bit here in the summer 'cause after Labor Day, all hell's gonna break loose again, and I'll be up against it." I said, "Okay. You come in for a ball game...." He said, "I've got to run." I said, "Me, too. I'll see you in a while." He said, "Okay. Take care, Bergy." That was our last conversation...our final words.

> He said, "Okay. Take care, Bergy."

I still am not able to get rid of his cell phone number in my speed dial; I just don't have it in me yet to whack it. Tim was literally the most loyal guy and friend you ever saw. He was extremely Catholic also. He got to be more of that as he grew older. He also took a decided turn to the right politically. He was very, very liberal when we were in college together. He was extremely against the Vietnam War. He was extremely against ROTC, which we had to take. He was pretty loud. I just went along for the ride, but he was really Left. He took a decided turn to the Right later. But, Tim stayed more Catholic, and he did not like it when people would do stuff that was out of the normal routine of what you would call a practicing Catholic. Tim and I used to party a lot together. I don't think either of us ever got arrested for anything. We probably should have, but we didn't. It was typical twenty-, twenty-one-, twenty-two-year-old college stuff.

One of my buddies asked me recently how I was doing. I said, "I'm doing okay. I'm trying to take this attitude: I met Tim in September of 1968. He died in June of 2008. I knew him as a very good friend for almost forty years—as close to forty as you are going to get." I knew him longer than his wife did, not to pick on Maureen. I don't say that I was closer. I'm just saying that I knew him that long. I knew Tim forty of the fifty-eight years he was around here, and we were very close friends. We did a lot of stuff together. I don't know what else to say.

Tim and I went to the Kentucky Derby our freshman year. I went every year, and Tim kept shaking his head and saying, "That one year was enough for me." In 1969, we drove down together. We probably each had about $70 in our pockets. We slept at the University of Louisville. We never got a hotel room. You got in for five bucks. Back then, you could take coolers in…with beer or anything you wanted to take in. We had our cooler packed, and we'd go to the infield. It was what you would think nineteen-year-old kids would be doing in the infield. It got crazier after that 'cause I kept going. After I had a couple of kids, my wife said, "We aren't going to the Derby any more. We've got to be a little more responsible."

One year we went to Notre Dame when they were playing USC, and the USC cheerleaders showed up. They're always the prettiest girls. I can't stand the school, but their cheerleaders are pretty.

Our sophomore year, I was a de facto roommate with Tim. Pat Hoak went to Canisius with Tim. He was severely diabetic. We were the only students on campus who were allowed a refrigerator 'cause Pat had to have insulin and had to keep it refrigerated, so we had one of those small refrigerators. Tim would always stop by our room 'cause he lived about three blocks off campus in a house. After a while, Tim

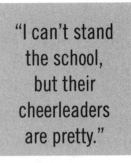

"I can't stand the school, but their cheerleaders are pretty."

would say, "Hoakie, you got to get rid of some of this insulin 'cause you're taking up all our beer room." Pat got really sick one time, and he had to spend about three months in the infirmary. Tim said, "S---, I'm moving in. I ain't walking to campus anymore. I'm taking Hoakie's place." So, when I say he was my roommate, it was a de facto situation, but, he was—he lived with me for ten months.

One day, Tim, being the knucklehead that he was, told me, "I just came back from the administration building, and I told the janitor who was there cleaning that I'd forgotten something in Father Woefl's office. 'I need you to open up the room for me.' The janitor opens up Father Woefl's office, and, sure enough, there was the final exam. So I copied it, and I've got the final exam right here." So, the day of the final comes, and it's the same test. It was one of those bluebook finals. We're just doodling. I'm doing tic-tac-toe there 'cause I'd already filled it out. I had a C+ going into the course and Tim had a B+ going in. The grades came. He calls me up and asks, "Hey, did you get your A in Woefl's class?" I go, "No, I got a C." So I call up Father Woefl and go, "Father this is Marty Bergerson. I got my grade and I got a C in this course. I couldn't have done better on the final exam if I had had the test ahead of time." Of course, which I did. He said, "Let me read it again and see." So, he called me back the next day and he said, "I re-read your exam and you are right. You did very, very well on that. I'm sorry. I'm going to move your grade to a B+." I said, "Thank you very much." I called Tim back and he said, "You didn't really tell him you couldn't have done better if you had had the test ahead of time?" I said, "That's exactly what I told him."

> "...I couldn't have done better on the final exam if I had had the test ahead of time."

Tim and I were taking a history course together. The history teacher was Dr. Howard, and she was blind—she had a seeing-eye dog. She knew her stuff and she was our teacher. At the final exam, Tim said, "How many tests you got left?" I said, "I only have one left—Howard's test tomorrow." I told him I really had to stay up and make sure I did well on it. About seven-thirty at night, Tim comes walking into my room. He goes, "Did you hear the news?" I said, "I didn't hear anything, Tim. What's up?" He goes, "Dr. Howard fell down the steps of the Ad building and there's no final. It's canceled and whatever grade you've got is the grade you get." I said, "Oh, WOW, off to the bar I am going." Sure enough, off to the bar I go getting drunk as s--- and at about 11:30 at night, these girls go, "Bergy, I thought you had a history test tomorrow." I said, "I did, but Dr. Howard fell down and the final has been canceled." They said, "Who told you that?" I said, "Russert did." They go, "Well, doesn't Russert have the test, too, tomorrow." I go, "Yeah." They said, "Well, where is he?" I said, "I don't know. He's probably out drinking somewhere else." They said, "No, he was BS-ing you." I said, "No way." I turned pale, and they said, "You've got a test tomorrow, buddy." I said, "Oh s---!" He always got me with stuff like that. I was ready to kill him. All he did was laugh. He said, "If you're stupid enough and gullible enough to believe me without looking into it...." I think I ended up getting a C or something.

That's the type of shenanigans Tim would pull or I would pull or we would pull together! Those aren't dirty stories. They're just knuckle-lehead stories. They're stories of life and fun and buddies. They're not really legal, but they're not really that illegal either. They're just fun stuff.

> "They're not really legal, but they're not really that illegal either. They're just fun stuff."

Tim's girlfriend was a wonderful gal named Lucy in those days. She was from Buffalo. That was one of the reasons he moved off-campus after freshman year. Back then at John Carroll you had some pretty restrictive guidelines, especially living in the dorms. Tim really liked his female companions so if he had an apartment, which he did, they didn't care as long as you paid the rent.

Tim was in my wedding. One winter he came in for a speech and we were drinking and he asked, "How many years have you been married?" I said, "Twenty-four now, and it'll be twenty-five next August." He goes, "Didn't you honeymoon on the East Coast?" I said, "Yeah, we went to Nantucket for eleven to twelve days." He goes, "I bought a home in Nantucket. This summer, plan on coming up for your twenty-fifth anniversary, and you and Susie can spend a week at the house. You can have your own little love cottage there." I said, "Thank you. That's awful nice of you." I didn't say anything to my wife 'cause I didn't want to call him out on it later. So about April, I got this phone call, and it was Tim. He said, "Hey Bergy, I'm setting up my summer schedule. I didn't forget about the invitation. I'm taking two weeks off—one in July and one in August. When did you get married?" I said, "August." Tim said, "I want you to come in August. My family is coming in July, and it'll be better in August." I said, "Okay, we'll come in August. Now, Tim, are you sure?" He said, "I'm telling you to come.

"Just don't drink me out of all my Rolling Rock."

We got an eight-bedroom, nine-bath house here in Nantucket. I want you and Susie to come out. What does she drink?" I said, "I drink Rolling Rock, and she drinks Bud Light." He goes, "Great. I drink Rolling Rock, too so I don't even have to buy more of that. Just don't drink me out of all my Rolling Rock." I said, "Don't worry. I won't."

I go home and tell my wife that Tim Russert has invited us for out twenty-fifth anniversary to his home in Nantucket. She said, "Come on. Quit bull-s------- me." I said, "No. No. No. Plus, we're going to a Red Sox game on Thursday, going down to the Cape on Friday, and we're staying until Tuesday. Then we'll come back up to Boston and fly back to Chicago." She said, "Come on." I said, "No. No. Tim wants to do it. All we've got to do is pay for the airfare. The rest of the trip, we have free accommodations." It was just such a nice treat that he never forgot the little things in life. When he talked to me in November about our anniversary and found out it was to be our twenty-fifth anniversary, he said, "I was at your wedding. Why don't you come on out? Maureen and I would love to have you." My wife still talks about it. That's what a great friend he was. It was a great four or five days. We were partying and drinking and horsing around and talking about old stuff. Every time we'd go out to dinner, because everyone knew who he was, he'd call and make the reservation. You tried to be unobtrusive, but you could see that everyone was staring at you.

On the way into the restaurant, we go through the kitchen to get in and it was like the scene from *Goodfellas* where the guy would walk through the kitchen to get into the bar because of the fact that there was a line out front, but he knew how to get in. They had a table waiting for him. It was just good times and fun.

We have a neat Carroll classmate in Chicago named Mark Pacelli. He's a very successful commodity broker-trader and he owns a piece of this company called Iowa Grain. They have a corporate jet. After Tim died, the next day, on Saturday morning,

Mark and I were playing golf and he said, "Bergy, I'm trying to get the corporate jet, but it's in Florida, and I don't know if I'll be able to get it up here, but I'll know later." On Sunday morning, he calls and said, "We've got it. It seats eight and you fill out the other four seats because I don't care who goes. You know who to put on the plane. We'll have to meet at Lockport Air Field at four-thirty in the morning and we'll come back that night."

On the flight, we talked about Tim's stupid little yellow Gremlin. He got it cheap, and probably by the time he got done with it, it was ready for the scrap yard. It was just a cheap car for transportation for him. Tim was pretty tight with his money, so he drove that car a long time. As they say, Tim had his First Communion money. He spent money when he went out, and I'm not saying he was cheap, but he wasn't throwin' away money. As far as he was con-

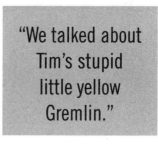

"We talked about Tim's stupid little yellow Gremlin."

cerned then, a new car would be p------ away money. It was just transportation to him. I'll bet the only time Tim drove a car was when he was in Nantucket. When I was in Nantucket a few years ago, he was driving around in a Jeep Cherokee convertible thing. He could have had whatever he wanted. They did have another family car that Maureen would drive. Tim always got a limo to drive him when he traveled. He didn't want to put himself into harm's way by having a few beers and then driving.

We land at Dulles and get on a limo bus to go about two blocks. Two classmates flew in from Boston. Off we go to the church, then twenty-two of us go to lunch at the Sequoyah Restaurant on the Potomac River. The next table over Ronan Tynan, the Irish tenor who sang "Ave Maria" at the funeral, just as he had for the funeral of President Reagan in 2004. When he sang "Danny Boy," well, to say I was a puddle would be putting it mildly. I knew I was going to be a wreck...I just didn't know how bad a wreck.

We had a great lunch. The restaurant was within walking distance of the Kennedy Center, so we just walked over there for the service. All of us John Carroll knuckleheads were in there together. I sat on fourth row, center. Three of us are walking up the aisle to leave. Andrea Mitchell, Alan Greenspan and me! They peel off to the right, and I had to go to the john, so I go to the men's room. I wasn't paying attention as I walked in...to my left is Tom Brokaw...to my right is Bill Clinton. I'm not lying to you. I said to myself, "You know what, Bergy, you didn't do too bad for a knucklehead from Michigan City. You're peeing next to a couple of heavy hitters! My mom would be so proud."

> **"...to my left is Tom Brokaw... to my right is Bill Clinton."**

Then, we went to the reception, which was held on the rooftop of the Kennedy Center. It was pretty crowded inside with all the people from Washington. I knew there had to be another place to go. I sneak around back and, sure enough, there's an outdoor patio with an open bar, all the food. I go in and say, "Come on guys. Follow me. Let's go." We're outside, overlooking the Potomac River. That's when we saw the double rainbow. The song they had played as they were bringing the casket out of the church was Israel Kamakawiwo'ole singing *Over the Rainbow.* It was so surreal. I thought, "Tim, I knew you were good, but now you've got a double rainbow here! What the hell are you doing? You're giving me the heebie-jeebies." If you told people, they wouldn't believe you— they'd think you were making it up. I experienced it first-hand. I just sat there and said, "You know what? Tim's got to be in heaven."

I haven't seen a double rainbow since I was in Waterville, Ireland playing golf four years ago. I was playing with my brother, my brother-in-law and a nephew. It rained real quick, and then a double rainbow showed up. I said to my brother-in-law, Mike Kelly, "You know what, Mike. The good Lord can almost take me now. Here I am playing golf in Waterville, Ireland, and I get a double rainbow I'm staring at. I don't know how it gets any better."

Then, when I saw the one at Tim's service, I just sat there saying, "This is just nuts! How do you have *Over the Rainbow* as they carry the casket out of the church and then there's a double rainbow over the Potomac?" It was weird. I had goosebumps.

We did all that. Luke Russert shows up and sees all of us John Carroll guys. He goes, "Where's Uncle Bergy?" He ran over and gave me a big hug. We talked and I told him, "Hey pal, I'm definitely coming to the Notre Dame-BC game in November in Boston." He goes, "You're damn right you're coming. I'll send the posse after you if you don't show up."

> "...that I got a Notre Dame degree, but an Ivy League education."

Tim did a commencement address at Notre Dame in 2002, when he was given an honorary degree. Tim ended his speech with, "You've got to understand. Here I am, a white, Irish Catholic kid from Buffalo, New York. Everyone loves Notre Dame. You know what? My dad is so proud of me. I now have a degree from Notre Dame, and, guess what? I got a Jesuit education." That was his parting line. I don't know if that went over very well with the Holy Cross fathers at Notre Dame. That's just the way Tim was.

To tell you the truth, though, he stole the line from John Kennedy because that's what John Kennedy used when he gave a speech at Notre Dame at a commencement address, "...that I got a Notre Dame degree, but an Ivy League education."

Because he gave the commencement address, he's what is called a legacy member at Notre Dame. He called me up the following spring, "Hey, they just sent me a notice that I can get two tickets for any sporting event I want. I have to pay for them." I said, "Buy the football tickets. We can always use more tickets." He bought them, sent them to me, and I sent him a check. Him being a legacy member and also being Tim Russert, these seats were all in Section 10, all the time, right on the fifty, on the visiting side. I said, "This is better than sex, for cripes sake, knowing this guy."

Last year, in August, I called him up and said, "Hey, Tim, you haven't called me about how much I owe you for the tickets." He said, "When I come out for the B.C. game, I'll give you the whole story." If you remember, last year is when they did those PSL/rental agreements at Notre Dame Stadium. They sent Tim a letter saying they were changing the format of legacy member status. "You're still a legacy member, but we are looking for a donation based on what we think you can afford and, Mr. Russert, we think that a contribution to the University of Notre Dame for $100,000 would allow you to continue to buy two tickets for every game." This is the straight story—Tim told me this in October! He goes, "Bergy, I really like this school. I didn't go to Notre Dame. My kid didn't go to Notre Dame. My dad didn't go to Notre Dame. I went to John Carroll. I know it's *the* Catholic University, but they can....I ain't sending them $100,000 for the opportunity to buy two tickets to every game. I've already got so many charities now. Forget it. So that's why you haven't been getting the two tickets this year. I wanted to tell you in person."

> "Sometimes, it's about friendships, loyalty and having a good time."

Luke is a great kid. NBC just hired him to be a news reporter for NBC for the election and some other things. He's a natural. He's really, really a good kid! He's very grounded. He probably only introduces himself as "Luke"—doesn't even introduce himself as "Luke Russert." He calls me Uncle Bergy, and he's a good family friend. I'm the knucklehead, but people like that. I try to not take myself so seriously. Do I like to be serious? Yeah. But you know what? Life's so short. It's not all about worry...about how much money I make....Sometimes, it's about friendships, loyalty and having a good time.

Tim loved my mother. Occasionally, he spent a night when we grew up in Michigan City, Indiana. When my mother turned sixty, Tim had Daniel Patrick Moynihan, who grew up in Hell's Kitchen, New York, send her a hand-written birthday note. Her maiden name is Duggan, and she's from County Cork...you'd have thought that she had gotten a letter from Jesus Christ. That made her day!

WOODSTOCK:
IT WAS A FOOLPROOF PLAN AND
THEY WERE THE FOOLS THAT PROVED IT!

Bill Brown

In a span of three weeks in late summer of 1969, there were several history-making events: Man walked on the moon, the Manson murders, Ted Kennedy drove off a bridge, and there was a little music festival called Woodstock. Bill Brown was two years ahead of Tim Russert at Canisius and John Carroll, but he and Russert forged a lifelong bond on a trip to Woodstock. Brown is a top executive with AARP in Atlanta. He served as a pallbearer at Tim Russert's funeral.

Tim and I were both working in Buffalo during the summer of 1969. We had to go back to Carroll at the end of August. We had talked about quitting a week or two early and finding something to do—go to the beach, go to the shore, do something. I can remember in July or early August hearing ads on the radio for this Woodstock concert, telling how tickets were available. I bought five weekend tickets, which cost $10 to $20 each for the weekend. I still have my ticket. Tim was still kicking himself for not having his and he would try to bribe me every time I saw him to give him my ticket. He wanted to give it to Luke, who has quite a collection of memorabilia. After I had the tickets, I convinced my mother to let me take her Valiant station wagon. We grabbed three other guys who were friends of mine who also knew Tim. We had read or heard a little bit about all the angst of the logistical problems the promoters were having.

We didn't have a real feel for what it was. We just figured there's going to be a bunch of people there—maybe thirty to forty thousand people. And some girls. One of the guys who came with us was working for the summer at a Loblaw's, one of the supermarket chains in New York. We got my mother's car and, at midnight, we left right from Loblaw's. We backed the car right up to the dock. He loaded us up with cold cuts, bread, beer, chips, mustard, catsup—all the provisions.

My mother's family is from Connecticut, so we'd made that drive a lot of times. You'd go down to Syracuse and cut through what was called the "quick way," Route 17 out of Binghampton, cutting right through the Catskills. My father is in the harness racing business, so I knew we got off right where the Monticello harness track raceway is. I knew it would take about four hours to get there and then maybe another forty-five minutes to get to Woodstock. We got to Exit 17B about four-fifteen in the morning. We made the turn, went about a mile or two on 17B, came up this hill...and as we crested this hill, all you saw ahead was brake lights. I remember passing the sign to White Lake—we were ten miles away...it took us three hours to go the next ten miles. Those poor people who lived on that road who woke up needing to go to work.... It was a two-lane highway, and they finally took both lanes and the shoulder on the right side so they had three lanes of traffic going toward White Lake and they allowed people trying to get out of there, the shoulder on the left side.

> "After three hours, we still weren't quite there."

After three hours, we still weren't quite there. People were beginning to pull off and park in open fields. We didn't even have a tent and had planned to sleep in or under the car. We pulled off in an open-field area and someone told us we were a mile or so from the site. By the time we had parked the car, it was seven or seven-thirty Friday morning. We decided to eat something, look around and walk over to see the place.

Now it's about nine o'clock. We walked down 17B, and there was a dirt road back into where the site was. You couldn't see anything from the road, so you had no idea. As we came into the clearing, there it was. There were not that many people around, but what struck me, and I can still remember, is the stage. It was nowhere near done. You could just look around and think, "How are they ever going to finish this?" There were people working, pounding nails and saws going. We hung around all day. You had the hog farm and there were people there who'd been there for days. You had people who were a lot different from us. I tell people that we were the straightest arrows I encountered. The concert was supposed to start that night at seven or eight o'clock...and it did. Richie Havens came out first. We took any food or drink we wanted to in with us. What struck us was that there was no admission gate. The promoters must have realized there was no way they were going to be able to take up tickets. I don't know if there was a record of how many tickets they actually sold compared with how many people showed up, whether it was 400,000 or 500,000. I believe they didn't sell any more than 50,000. That's why everybody still has their ticket...nobody took them up. There was no gate. There was no entrance. There was just a walk down the road...into the field...into a semi-circle of a bowl with a stage at the bottom and a lake behind that. It was chaos.

> "That's why everybody still has their ticket...nobody took them up."

We hung around all day and had great seats. That was "folk" night, so to speak. I've got an original poster up on my wall here in the office. That night was Joan Baez, Arlo Guthrie, Tim Hardin, Richie Havens, the Incredible String Band, Ravi Shankar, Sly and the Family Stone, Sweetwater, Bert Summer—folk night. It week-ended into the harder stuff and more rock and roll. We were probably thirty or forty feet from the front of the stage. We'd gotten there early so we just went down and staked out our ground. We left that night and went back to the car to sleep.

You had a sense, that first day, that this was really something. I didn't expect nearly this many people...or the kind of people who were there. We saw hard-core. If you had a picture in your mind of Haight-Ashbury and had never been there, it would have been transferred in some ways to right there in the middle of upstate New York at this farmer's dairy farm.

Over the weekend, we saw three or four guys we knew. Everything there was just on your own—whatever you could find. We'd walk back and forth past this farmhouse that had a swimming pool in the backyard. When we went back for Saturday's show, the closest we could get was about one-third to one-half way down the hillside. You weren't as close. If you see the movie or see the daytime shots with everybody packed into that natural ampitheater, we were probably about halfway down, as opposed to the night before, when we were two or three rows from the front of the stage.

> "But it rained. When it rained, there was no cover."

But it rained. When it rained, there was no cover. It was fun for a while, but then it got miserable. We decided that night that when we went back to the car that we would jump into the swimming pool. It was one or two in the morning and the people who lived there had left. We don't know if they planned to leave, but, with all the chaos around them, they got outta Dodge. There were no lights there, but we'd seen the pool when we'd walked by the farmhouse three or four times so we jumped in. Well, the next morning, we're walking by it in daylight. This pool was filthy. It looked like an oil slick. What Russert told Brokaw was that it was used as a bathroom. It wasn't so much that, it was the people who'd gotten so filthy dirty in the rain on that muddy hillside. So unbeknownst to us, we weren't the only ones who used it...and we may not have been the first.

On stage, Arlo Guthrie said, "The New York Thruway is closed, man." Because there were so many people coming up from the city, they shut down the freeway. That was late Saturday morning, so by then we had a pretty good idea that this was a special event. On the radio, you heard these wild estimates that there were 250,000 and then 400,000. All we could think about was, "What do you supposed our parents are hearing? Or, what are they thinking?"

It was warm rain, and we got sick of the weather. It turned the ground into a quagmire. It was very difficult to enjoy yourself because it was just mud everywhere. You had that side of the hill so everything ran down.

Finally, on Sunday night, the acts were really backed up because of delays from the rain. They were trying to build up to the great acts: Crosby, Stills and Nash, Jimi Hendrix and The Who. They were all supposed to have been Sunday afternoon and evening. The weather had backed up everything so much that it was going to be really late when they performed. To tell you the truth, we were so miserable by Sunday night that we threw in the towel. We left at around nine or ten o'clock Sunday night and decided to drive to New Jersey where another one of our classmates lived. We'd decided we were going to head to Washington, D.C., because it would be a good way station. We didn't want the fun to end—we wanted to keep it going. We had all quit our jobs to take the last week or two before going back to school.

We had some money. We had my mother's car. She, to her dying day, claims that we didn't tell her about the Washington part. My parents were looking to get the car back.

We drove to a Howard Johnson's somewhere in suburban New Jersey, which was not far from where our classmate lived. People had been leaving in waves, and a lot stayed around, but traffic was not too bad when we left and we didn't have any trouble getting out. Looking back, it all ended at about dawn on Monday when Hendrix did the "Star Spangled Banner" and, comparatively speaking, there weren't many people left there. Seems like most people left Sunday afternoon/ Sunday night, depending on how much staying power you had.

> "We didn't want the fun to end—we wanted to keep it going."

One of the guys flew home to Michigan and the four of us drove a couple of hours to the motel. Then, we called home. At some point, there was relief for our parents. They were convinced that we were stoned, which they didn't want to think. Actually, none of us did any weed or anything. We really were pretty straight. We did drink a lot of beer. In my case what happened was my dad's business partner died in his sleep a few days earlier. Of course, they called my father at home, and he thought it was me. In a perverse way, that helped me. They were so relieved that wasn't "the call," so that when I did call, they weren't screaming. I told them we were going to go to Washington to see some sights. I'd been there before but that was Russert's first trip to Washington. It's ironic that Tim came back and made such a name for himself there twenty years later.

He said, "Do you mind if we look around outside?"

In Washington, we had a great time. After we'd stayed overnight and spent some time on Monday with this classmate in New Jersey, we decided to drive down. About halfway down, Russert says, "You know, remember that girl, Dana Cohen, from Lake Erie College?" This was a college near the John Carroll campus. Her father ran a huge supermarket chain in the D.C. area. She lived in a condo across from the Shoreham on Calvert Street there. Russert said, "We've got to call her. We can stay with her." We said, "We can't stay with her. That's not the right thing to do." Russert said, "She'll be fine. She's not living with her parents." We called her when we got out the outskirts of D.C. She said, "Sure, come on over and stay with me." Here are the four of us guys staying with this single girl...and she was a knockout...she was gorgeous. Years later, Russert would still talk about the wraparound skirts she wore. We used that condo like it was our home base, and we did everything. We went to the Capitol. We met Everett Dirksen, who was the minority leader at the time. For some reason, he brought us into his office, where we could look out his window right down the mall. We had both worked for Bob Kennedy. Charles Goodell was in the Senate seat then as a temporary replacement for him. His son, Roger Goodell, is now the commissioner of the NFL. We rode the underground train and walked around the Mall. One of the coolest thing we did—we wanted to find Hickory Hill 'cause we were such Kennedy devotees, and we had worked for Bobby Kennedy.

We found Hickory Hill. Russert said, "Pull in." We parked in front and walked right up to the front door and rang the bell. It was late August now. Russert planned to tell them that he had seen Ted Sorenson, and Ted Sorenson said we should stop by and say hello. The maid came to the door and Russert told her this. I got out my little Brownie camera and was standing there. I honestly thought Russert was going to say, "Do you mind if we come in...?" But he didn't. He said, "Do you mind if we look around outside?" We went around back to the pool and saw where they kept their pony. I took pictures of the pool and the cabana house. The funny thing is, twenty years later, Andrew Cuomo married Mary Kerry Kennedy, and that's where the reception was—on the grounds at Hickory Hill—and Russert went back. Russert and I were in heaven because of the way we felt about the Kennedys. It was not as big a thrill to the other two guys.

We went to a Washington Senators game. Ted Williams was the manager. They were awful. If it wasn't their last year in D.C., it was their second-to-last year. They moved to Texas and became the Texas Rangers. It was an afternoon game. Naturally, we had to have beer with us—we weren't going to pay the prices at the ball park. It's summertime. How are you going to sneak in beer? They caught us. Russert made a deal with the guy at the turnstile, "How about if we just keep the beer here, and when we want one, we'll come back here and drink it in front of you?" The guy says okay—can you believe that? Only Russert would have the gall to even think of asking that. We get in and our seats are down the first-base line. There may be five or six thousand people there. Russert had been saying all morning,

> "Only Russert would have the gall to even think of asking that."

"I'm going to get a foul ball." Tim spends half the time ragging Williams. Finally there's a pop fly down the right field line, and, of course, there's no one there so it's a sprint to get to the ball. Russert did. He got it. We had to run some interference for him 'cause he wasn't the fastest guy. I was faster, but he was closer to where it started out. In life, he seemed to do a lot of the things he said he would. It's nuts, but it happens.

> His reference was, "Brown went to Woodstock with me."

Tim and I had only been real close friends at that point eight or nine months. That trip to Woodstock and Washington was what made our friendship solid. One time, two years ago, when I went to *Meet the Press*, the guest was one of the guys from Springsteen's band. When the taping was over, there are usually only ten to fifteen people there to watch the taping, sitting on folding chairs. Tim would come over and pose for some pictures. Then, if he knows you, you'd go up on the set and he'd hang around. On this day, I had my sister and her husband, who had known Tim for a long time, and a woman from work. Tim made sure we got to go over and meet the guy from his band. His reference was, "Brown went to Woodstock with me." To this guy, that's a click—"bingo" for him. When my mother passed away, Tim came to the wake, and we all went back to the house afterward. Invariably, the Woodstock stories would start. There are a couple of things in Tom Brokaw's book that I think he, in typical Russert fashion, exaggerated a little bit. For one thing, I don't ever remember being in Buffalo Bills jerseys, and I don't remember tossing a football around that much. We might have. That was good stuff for him to tell Brokaw.

We had three nights in Woodstock and then a night in New Jersey, and then we had three or maybe four nights in D.C. We took Dana out to dinner Friday night, unloaded her, and then we went drinking. Around midnight, we left to drive back to Buffalo, a seven-hour drive, after eating dinner and drinking. We drove all the way back on the Pennsylvania Turnpike. We were so tired.

We got to West Seneca, and Tim's mother gave us breakfast. I drove home to Batavia, New York and probably got there around nine or ten o'clock Saturday morning. I do remember that my parents were so ------ at me, and I was so tired. Do you know what they made me do? That night, Saturday night, the Bills had an exhibition football game back in Buffalo. They made me take my younger brother to it. I was so tired...and they made me get a haircut.

Tim's father was working two jobs, and I remember that he was a little miffed at us over the whole Woodstock thing. He was a good guy and was also great to me, as was his mother.

Tim Russert—wow, what a guy!

SHORT STORIES FROM
LONG MEMORIES

All those things people said on TV about Tim...they're true... they're very true. I'm a high school teacher. I'm not in the circle that Tim moved in, and yet he had the time to talk and to ask how things had been going. My classic Tim Russert story happened about two years ago.

Tim was in Cleveland giving a talk for the kickoff the time when John Carroll was starting a scholarship for the inner-city kids. Tim was speaking at one of the downtown hotels. Someone had given our school a set of tickets so that anybody who wanted to could go at no expense and hear Tim talk. I jumped at the chance. I came into the hotel and was not sure which way to go. I take the escalator up and can't figure out how to get into this ballroom. One of the employees told me, "I'll take you through this way, and that will lead you through the deck room into the ballroom." There was another person there who was not a part of our school, and he directed all of us to follow him. I walked in. And, sitting there in the back eating his dinner before he goes to talk—Tim Russert. Right away, Tim said, "Hi Betty, how are things going? Are you coming to hear me talk?" He had not seen me in thirty years. This other person was just shocked and amazed. But this is what Tim Russert is like. He remembered his classmates. He remembered his ties to Carroll—they were very, very deep.

When Tim was at the reunion, the powers that be pulled him over to make a few videos, make a few bucks, but he also had time for the rest of us. I was always impressed by that about Tim.

Our graduating class at John Carroll is the first official coed class. There was one coed dorm. If you go to the John Carroll web page, somebody was talking about how they worked with Tim Russert to get an open dorm policy for our senior year. I always laughed when I would see Tim on TV and I would say, "I voted for

Tim for student union president. I helped him on his way to becoming this great political guru."

Tim always greeted everybody. At reunions, they would show pictures of Tim as he looked back in the early '70s, with the long hair, Fu Manchu mustache, the whole bit. People would go, "Who is that? That can't be Tim Russert." Oh yeah...that was Tim.

One of the men that Mike Barnicle spoke about, Dennis Quilty, was at the reunion. Quilty said he never bought a JCU yearbook for two reasons. He didn't buy it when we graduated because he didn't want his parents to see what he looked like. Then later, he didn't buy one because he didn't want his kids to see what he looked like. Those were the kind of people Russert hung around with.

I had some thoughts about whether or not Tim would run for public office, especially know-ing that he had worked for the politicians. I don't know, though, since he was living more and more in Washington, and was getting older. And what office would you run for after you've run *Meet the Press* and run the Washington NBC office? You don't run for city council in Buffalo! Hillary Clinton now is the senator from New York, so would he go back to New York? I always thought that possibly he would have run for office, but I don't know whether he would have done it unless it was some-thing for fun—run for school board or something after he retired.

He would have made a wonderful 'whatever.' Obviously he was very hard working. Tim was what the people say about him. You watched the TV and you heard all the comments about how Tim had done so many things and how he felt about so many things. To those of us who knew him as a kid, yes, Tim was all those things they said. He did have all these positive attitudes. He did love his faith, and he did love his school.

—<u>BETTY DABROWSKI</u>, Tim Russert's college classmate

I told the people I work with, "Everything you heard on television about Tim Russert was true." This isn't one of those made-up things. He really was the smartest person I knew in college. He was a real activist and, I think, really ahead of his time.

Tim was in the U-Club. I don't want to say he was aloof...but he was just smarter than the rest of us. A lot of those guys were just nitwits! They would party and party. Hopefully they've all grown up and gotten real jobs but, at the time, they were goofy. They were just partiers. Although he did party, Tim was always a little bit on the fringe because you got the idea he had bigger things in mind.

Everything you'd heard about Tim or read about him in that period was absolutely true. There wasn't one exaggeration. Tim thought deeper thoughts than the rest of us. That was a funny age...a funny era. At John Carroll we were very provincial. We were pretty secluded and a little bit sheltered. We weren't Berkeley. We weren't on the East Coast or on the West Coast—clearly in the Midwest. Football games and fraternity parties and that kind of stuff were the things we cared about....except Tim. He knew more—he cared about more things. Tim cared about things back then that we cared about when we got older. He was like an "old soul."

He would come to reunions. Their class was a year ahead of mine so it was their reunion, not mine, but I thought I would go up and see who was around. One time I got home from work on a Friday night, and the phone rang. I picked it up and answered it. This voice said, "Where the hell are you?" I said, "Who is this?" He said, "It's Tim Russert." I said, "Yeah, really, who is it really?" He said, "No, it is Tim. Where are you?" I told him I had just come in, and he said, "We're at Nighttown. Get down here." So I did. I went down.

I work at the Cleveland Sight Center, and he said, "Oh man, that must be fascinating." "No, actually not. Considering that what you do is very fascinating." Tim was not like that. He was never one of those people who looked at you, but like he was looking over your shoulder to see if somebody better was coming along. He wasn't. He looked at you, and he was interested in you, not the more important person behind you. The first thing he asked was, "How are your kids? Do you have pictures? What are they doing? What are you up to?" Tim was really interested in your family and what you did. You would never have known that he was going to get picked up in the morning by a helicopter to be taken back to do *Meet the Press.*

When Tim came to the reunions, he didn't often stay all three days. He might just come in for a day or two. You would never have known that this was someone who had met presidents and kings and queens.

—SHARON BOWEN, John Carroll University, Class of '73

I remember Tim as an active individual. We had a building that has since been renovated, and I can still picture Tim in front of that building with other students. Those were the days when students were very active in regard to the hippie movement coming in, and the Vietnam War and the draft.

Tim was always a very warm individual. In fact, I was very surprised when he would come back to campus and I'd walk toward him, and I was ready to re-introduce myself, and he would say, "Hi, Father Bukala." Just a couple of years ago, Tim gave a talk at the Renaissance Center Hotel downtown. I walked up to him. Someone wanted to introduce me, and they said, "This is Father Bukala." He said, "Oh, I know."

I teach philosophy here. There's a philosopher, Soren Kierkegaard, who said we should live our life with passion. As chaplain, I used to share with the football team that what Kierkegaard meant by passion is that whatever you do, you do to the best of your ability. That's what Tim was really about. He may have been a regular John Carroll student whom I recall at alumni reunions with individuals gathered around him because he really shone among other people. He did everything to the best of his ability. He was also a very humble person. Tim didn't lord it over individuals, especially in a group such as his own classmates.

It was rather beautiful when you think of seeing someone who had really made it and was just standing around with his classmates and laughing and having a good time. He accepted them on the same level as he. All truly great people are humble people. Some people are considered great, but they are not as great as they

could be if they were humble. If a person is humble, that humility leads a person to become better and better and better. You're not at the finish line...but you're moving toward it. In a way, *Meet the Press* every Sunday was moving toward the finish line. There was not one Sunday presentation that would have been the best of all.

I can picture Tim's face from being very serious...to laughing. He was a good person. That's the greatest compliment that can ever be said about an individual.

—FR. CASEY BUKALA, philosophy teacher
for thirty-eight years at John Carroll

My fondest memory of Tim Russert was on Parents' Weekend. My dad was an attorney, a prosecutor, a judge and then ended up being a federal judge. At the gathering, instead of Tim partying with his friends, he and my dad would sit in a corner and talk politics. You couldn't separate the two of them. That was all Tim wanted to do. He couldn't have been more than twenty or twenty-one years old at the time. My dad's response at the end of the night was "Oh, I so thoroughly enjoyed meeting your friend. He's really going to go somewhere. I can see him in politics someday. What a bright young man...." You could tell he just had it in his blood. Later on, my dad would see Tim on television and he was so proud of him. Dad was big into "I told you so."

Tim was always a gentleman, always the nicest guy. They weren't all, but Tim always was. I have very fond memories of him. He was always friendly, very courteous, treated me like a lady. I went to the reunion ahead of mine because I always hung out with the guys in that class. There was Tim walking across campus *with his entourage following him—all those guys.* My image of Tim was him leading six or eight guys walking across the campus, almost like they were protecting him. These were the same friends he had in college and all were with him that reunion day.

Tim was always the perfect gentleman—that's how I remember him.

—DEBBIE LAVALLE, John Carroll University, Class of '73

Tim was a big man on campus, both literally and physically. He was a tall, big voiced, big personality, long hair, mutton-chop whiskers, fatigue jackets, bib overalls.

He would have been one of the first I met because he was one of the crew who welcomed the incoming students. In those days, there was a week of incoming activities before we started class, very unlike today. I was in the first group of women students to live on campus at Murphy Hall.

There was a 13:1 ratio our freshman year. By the time I graduated, four years later, it was 51% female students—fifty-fifty. It went coed very quickly. I'm sure that the only reason they went coed was financial in an attempt to boost enrollment. Those of us who went were there because it was a great school.

Particularly Tim's class, by coincidence, the class of 1972, was legendary for their cohesiveness, and their reunions are always the best. I crash them every opportunity I get because they are very well attended. I have many friends in that group, one year ahead of ours. We gathered the week after Tim's funeral and celebrated our thirty-fifth reunion for the class of '73. Tim Russert was the main topic of conversation, and the stories were charging around the dinner table all weekend.

Tim was universally loved. Not a single person who knew Tim Russert in college has been at all surprised by the path his life took. Not a one. He was that way in school. He was curious about everyone. He was passionate about the issues of the day. He was a pacifist. He was an anti-war activist. He was always after what was true—what was your truth? If he was talking to you—in what was true for you. In a conversation with Tim Russert, you didn't beat around the bush. You weren't coy. You didn't evade the question. He wanted straight answers. We all are better communicators for having known him.

I don't remember Tim having a main squeeze. That doesn't mean he didn't have one, but I don't remember anyone in particular. I do remember him going out with some of the gals on campus. We had all of those parties, and he was certainly a very good time.

The last time I saw Tim to talk to him face-to-face was when he was giving the commencement address at John Carroll in 1997. Also, he was picking up one of his dozens of honorary doctorates. It was brief 'cause he's a busy guy. We always think we have all the time in the world and it'll wait for the next reunion. Guess what?

—MARY ANN SPINKS-MILLER, Solon, Ohio, high school friend/
English teacher

You develop a friendship and a bond over time. After college, I hadn't seen Tim directly or talked with him until six years ago. He came into San Antonio to speak at Trinity University. Every year they bring in five speakers with some degree of notoriety, maybe from the business community or from the political arena. Tim was one of these speakers. I subscribed to those breakfast meetings for well over twenty years, probably closer to thirty years. Tim was there and I saw him as he came through the door. I said, "Hey Timmy." It was one of those deals where he looked at me—and the wheels are turning—and you're saying to yourself, "He looks familiar, but I don't know who...." Then, as I was saying, "Hey, I'm Steve," he said, "Steve Varga." We chatted for a few moments and talked about an individual by the name of Billy Brown. Bill was in my class and was from Buffalo. Apparently, Bill and Tim had stayed in close contact with each other, understandably so. Then, Tim went on to speak, and I went to my office.

I wasn't surprised that Tim remembered my name after all those years. Number one—he's a smart guy, and two—you spend time together over a period of three to four years. My looks haven't changed a lot, except that I have no hair on my head. As far as I'm concerned, hair is overrated.

On campus, Tim was highly energized with politics and he was very smart. We had some kind of mock political convention in '68. Various fraternities took the role of different candidates. Our fraternity chose Nelson Rockefeller. How we chose him—I have no idea. There were different positions you took. You had to do research. People were working different elements on the floor, and there were caucuses and that kind of thing that went on. It was on for an entire Saturday. It was energized, and Tim was involved. Afterward, we celebrated. I can't remember *what* we celebrated—I don't know whether we got Nelson Rockefeller elected or not. Afterward, we had a big party, and there was an old clay water-pipe there. Russert had found it in the road and brought it in, and we all wrote our names on it. That became part of the University Club symbol of something. Russert's dad would have shot him if he knew Tim was promoting Nelson Rockefeller.

Values are why we do things in life. If one has received the proper values, which I think Tim got from his parents and from the nuns who taught him, he carried that through. He never forgot a friend. He was always sensitive toward other people— just the hallmark of a terrific character.

I have to tell you that there are a lot of lessons that can be learned from someone like Tim Russert. It appears that nice, sensitive guys, despite the fact that at times they have to be able to position themselves and ask the right kind of questions can finish on top of the heap. John Carroll has a lot to be proud of and I know Buffalo does also. As a student of John Carroll, I am proud of that. Also, as a fraternity brother, I am most proud of the fact that I had just the opportunity to drink a few beers with the guy. I hope that I can display some of those characteristics to some of the people I work with.

—STEVE VARGA, 50, San Antonio, Texas

There is an annual fundraising, charity dinner for student scholarships for journalism called the Gridiron Dinner. It's an opportunity where the governor and administration pre-record skits that poke fun at themselves. Then the media will do skits that poke fun at themselves. It's all in really good fun, similar to the White House Press Corps dinners.

One of the skits they did early on was with Governor Tom Ridge going on a mock *Meet the Press*. They had Tom Ridge being interviewed by Tim Russert. It was never aired, but it was shown at the fundraising dinner. It was really fun. That video shows Tim

Russert asking very pointed questions of Tom Ridge, poking fun at an early snafu in his administration. It was really fun to see the two of them play off of each other. It's a video that's not out there because it was never released to the public...but the dinner crowd went wild over it. I always think, what a great *Meet the Press* moment. Tim Russert was known for tough questions. Here was this hilarious video that played off that whole point that Tim was a tough interviewer, but a fair interviewer. It also shows a governor being excited about going on *Meet the Press.* Just by seeing Governor Ridge's personality come through, it was a really fun skit. It showed how they both had such good qualities of being very down to earth.

When people who have been working in politics or government are looking at Tim Russert, there's a term called "being Russert-ready." Could political candidates be ready to go on that show? If they're not ready and they are running just for the sake of being an elected official, then they would never stand up on Tim Russert's show because they're just not prepared. They don't know the issues. They don't know why they want to run. They aren't really ready to make an impact. I look at that as an example that Tim Russert "in that skit with Tom Ridge" played off of Tim Russert asking the tough questions, but in reality, Tim made a lot of people better and better candidates.

—MIKE GILDEA, assistant to one-time Pennsylvania governor Tom Ridge—later the director of Homeland Security

Tim was a social guy and a party guy. He loved to have a good time. We were a group of people who got along well together. We hung together. We probably over-imbibed together. Tim was dating Lucy, a girl from Buffalo, pretty regularly. She was a really neat person. Lucy would come in for spring weekend or homecoming, things like that. We got to know her really well.

After we were out of college, my grandmother, a down-home Irish cook in her late eighties, had a whole bunch of people over to their home for dinner. The story in my family still goes, "Oh my God, Tim ate so many potatoes." He was the "potato guy" from then on.

Tim really took a liking to my grandmother, who lived to age ninety-seven. At one point, Tim sent her a bunch of memorabilia from NBC, a cap, duffel bag and stuff. She really appreciated the fact that he would even take the time to think of her and do that because he was already on *Meet the Press*. She watched him on the show regularly. When Tim would see me, he would ask me how she was doing. I'd say, "Well, she's still alive and kicking." Then, a little while later, she got all these things in the mail from him.

—FR. BOB YTSEN, Jesuit priest, teacher at Loyola Academy, Chicago

The only thing Tim was completely biased about was the Buffalo Bills. I would watch Tim every single Sunday. I've taped him over here for as long as it's played over here. I might watch it on Wednesday or Thursday, but I taped him every week. For one big Bills game, he actually announced to the nation that God had intended the Bills to win that weekend. I can't remember his exact phrase, but I remember, at the time, I couldn't believe he said that on national television. That was the only thing on that program that was not well balanced. That was his choice of sports teams...and he was forgiven for that by both sides.

Tim loved baseball of any kind, and he had sports heroes who were from everywhere. But the odd thing about him is that he was the same way. He supported his community, no matter where he was. When he was in Cleveland, he was supporting the local producers and the local promoters to bring talent in there. Whatever sports were there, he followed them. Whatever charities were local, he did that.

I have a friend who didn't know Tim, but who wrote him a letter one time. Tim wrote him a nice personal check to support his boys' charity. He was a very generous guy and a very caring guy. If he liked the story you told about the charity and it was going to help a kid somewhere, he'd probably give you a few bucks. This was not publicized. This was not a big deal. He was always very quiet about it. He wasn't the kind of guy who would give you something and then want everybody to know about it. The real story about Tim is that he was genuine.

Everybody felt bad when Tim died—you would have thought John F. Kennedy had died if you had been watching the TV. The reason is that he touched everybody he came across. That was genuine. That was who he was.

I'm a salesman, so one of the things I noticed about Tim was that you can push a guy and push a guy and push a guy, but you don't want to push him over the edge. You want to push and keep asking and asking and asking, but not so much that he'll never talk to you again. I always noticed that in Tim. He always knew when to stop. He'd be relentless...and sometimes they wouldn't answer him, but he knew when to stop. Very rarely did I see him get sort of annoyed.

The only time I saw him get annoyed was one time when he was interviewing Colin Powell when Powell was in the Middle East. The picture went black. They had moved the camera away from Colin Powell. Timmy thought it was deliberate. Colin Powell could be heard in the background, "No, put it back here. He's still here. I can hear him. Put it back here. We're not finished." I think somebody pulled him away because the questions were getting hot. Timmy got annoyed because he didn't know who had done it and Colin Powell brought it back. It was a very interesting dialogue that was there.

—FRANK PALAMARA, London

We knew Tim for being Tim...not for being the guy on NBC. He loved that aspect of it. This political campaign was a big thing for him. He told my brother, "After the Indiana primary, and the North Carolina date, you're going to be watching the next president—not the nominee—Obama's going to be the next president."

We lived vicariously through Tim. Last October, when Tim came out for the Boston College-Notre Dame game, that was the last time I saw him. Luke was with him and we had an incredible time.

He loved going to the Cubs games. He always wanted to sit in the regular seats—didn't want to sit in the skyboxes. My brother has been a thirty-year ticket holder at the Cubs games and Tim liked to sit in his seats.

We got a lot of pictures of Tim the day of the Boston College-Notre Dame game. We were using NBC tickets for the game and my brother said that one seat was on the fifty and one on the forty-nine! My seats were just one section over, so we were throwing stuff back and forth to each other all day.

Walking places with Tim, people would all point. When we were in the parking lot tailgating, people would walk by, point and say hey. Some would ask to have their picture taken with him...he'd be very kind, generous and would do that and would be very accommodating. That day, he didn't really want to leave, but being on a Saturday, Tim had to get back to Washington for *Meet the Press.*

When I saw him last, he and my brother went to the limo at Notre Dame to take him back to the airport. He was just ordinarily dressed. Tim wore his food on his shirt all the time. In college, he was really sloppy. We always gave him a hard time about it.

Tim always had a lot of energy—I don't know how he did it. He was always on the go. I think that's what sports did for him—it gave him the opportunity to sit for a couple of hours and relax a little bit. There, he was in an area where he didn't have some of these outside extraneous things going on.

—MICHAEL BERGERSON, John Carroll '74

At college fairs and visits to high schools, we used to have "view books." They were like a prospectus you'd have for prospective students. I would have the page of one of the view books open with Tim Russert's picture very visible. These would always include a page on prominent alumni. I would always make it a point to have that part of the view book open on the table at college fairs. Of course, all the parents would recognize it right away and comment, "Oh, Tim Russert went to school here. You should consider this school." Most people who know him are aware that he had a background in politics, an expert in the field. If their son or daughter was thinking along the lines of political science, history, law, they would immediately put it all together—this must be a really nice place.

About five slides into the presentation there was a quote from Tim essentially saying, "You can read all the books...you can know all the facts...but the emphasis on ethics and values are what matter with an education. How are you going to use this education to serve the community? That's what makes the difference at John Carroll. That's what makes John Carroll distinctive." It was always the slide that came up either after or before the core curriculum. "This is what we do. You'll have a core curriculum and you'll have your major, but this is the extra piece that makes us special and makes us stand out." Of course, that had a lot of credibility because Tim's name was associated with it.

—DAN BUTLER, former admissions counselor at John Carroll University

I was three years ahead of Tim Russert at John Carroll. I first met Tim in my senior year when I was president of Young Democrats. It was 1968, and Tim was real involved in the Humphrey election.

My first real passion and livelihood is real estate, and my second passion is politics so Tim and I had a lot in common going way back. Clearly the guy on TV that everybody saw was the guy that I knew. I think that is what made him so popular. His whole demeanor was the same one-on-one as it was in front of millions of people. Most people in public life or on television aren't able to get that across to the screen, but Tim was not a faker and he was just a great straight-shooter. He was very insightful about everything he did in life.

—HOWARD "HODDY" HANNA, real estate tycoon, Pittsburgh and Cleveland

Chapter 3

Marshall Law School

A Good Lawyer Knows the Law, A Great Lawyer Knows the Judge

TAKE THIS JOB AND LOVE IT

Marie Colette Gibbons

Marie Colette Gibbons has known Tim Russert since her first day as a freshman at John Carroll University. The Canton, Ohio native spent the next seven years sharing classes and laughter with Russert through law school. She is partner--in-charge of the Cleveland office of Schottenstein, Zox & Dunn.

I was in the first-ever class of women admitted to John Carroll. There were seventy-three of us on the Carroll campus in those days. Four of us from Canton went to Carroll from our high school. We had each other. We weren't too scared. We were annoyed from time to time because some of the men at the campus weren't very accepting. We enjoyed being so few girls among a whole campus of boys. Those were good years.

Some of the guys at John Carroll would make fun of us girls and how we looked. We were in skirts all the time, and some of them were a little rude. For the most part, I think we fit in pretty well after a year to a year-and-a-half.

After Tim graduated from John Carroll, he went back to Buffalo for a year. He wasn't really sure he wanted to go to law school. Those were tumultuous times. Nobody was thinking like, "Oh, I'm going to be a corporate lawyer." Everybody was thinking—"social justice and what can I do for the world." So, politics seemed to be a noble calling. I'm not sure what office Tim worked in during that year—county attorney, maybe but he shared an office with a guy named Frank Szuniewicz. Szuniewicz—pronounced "zen-oh-wits"—referred to himself as "Frankie Sonofabitch" because people were always mispronouncing his name.

Frank Szuniewicz loaned Tim $2,000 to go back to school. It was money that Frank won in a card game. I wrote about it in one of the speeches when I would introduce Tim in Cleveland. I remember Tim saying he didn't know what to do with the money...so he put the money in the freezer—his first experience with "cold cash."

When I showed up at Marshall Law school the first day—and back then, it wasn't a prestigious law school. It is now. It's a marvelous school now. But back then, they had some not-so-great professors. I loved, loved, loved the people I went to school with, but I just think the some of the professors were a little bit silly. This was after John Carroll, where I'd had great teachers. Nobody at John Carroll had intimidated us or did the cross-examination stuff.

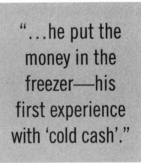

"...he put the money in the freezer—his first experience with 'cold cash'."

We showed up in law class the first day, it was ridiculous. The professors were trying to cut people down...and this isn't the only law school that is like that. The first day of school, I saw Tim in the student lounge area, which was a horrible room. It was a mess. He started making fun of these guys, making fun of school. "What are we doing here? We could be doing...." I'm laughing, and thinking, "This is going to be fun. He's here. We're going to have a good time." And *we did*. We just had a blast.

Tim was a hustler so he always seemed to have a little more money than the rest of us. We were all—as my mother always said—"church poor." We didn't have any money. I had three sisters behind me, and Tim had sisters coming up, and our parents didn't have any money. We had to hustle in law school with all kinds of jobs.

With some of these ridiculous professors, we developed a system for Tim not having to go to class. He would stand outside the class and read the *New York Times*. If the professors got close to the "*Rs*," or I thought there was any chance he was going to get called on, then I would signal him to come into the classroom. I was sitting in a position where I could motion for him to come in, and he would. It was a big-sized class so we got away with it.

> "*All* of us knew that he was never going to practice law."

That was what Tim wanted to do back then—read newspapers. In between classes, we'd go down to the Cleveland Public Library and Tim would read the newspapers from all over the country. He'd say, "This is a nationally recognized library. This is very cool that we can come down here." That's where his heart was all three years. *All* of us knew that he was never going to practice law. It was a skill set that Tim wanted, and that's why he went to law school. I heard him say in some of his talks that he thought he might go back to Buffalo and practice law or be a judge or something like that. At no time did I think he would do that. I thought he would go into politics. Not journalism—politics.

Tim was dating a girl in Buffalo our first year of law school. Tim and Mark would go out with girls, but I wasn't around for that. Tim would wear jeans that he couldn't keep up. He wore tee shirts. He often had a beard. He would be much, much heavier than he was recently. Then he would go on a diet and lose thirty pounds in a month. He's just would quit drinking beer, eat salads and the weight would fall off of him.

Tim cracked the code of law school. One of the things the professors would do would be to bind old exams for use as study aids. If you were taking "Wills and Trusts" you could go to the library and see exams for the last five years and study from that. One day, Tim raised his hand and asked the teacher, "Professor, you've written this wonderful article. I was wondering whether or not you'd ever taught at any other law school?" The professor said, "As a matter of fact, I taught at the University of Akron." "Did you teach this course there, professor?" "Yes, I did." Tim turned to me and said, "Road trip!"

So, we flew down to Akron in Tim's sawed-off Gremlin, giggling all the way. We'd sure rather have been doing this than sitting there studying. When we got to Akron, we went to the law library, where they also kept bound copies of previous years' tests. We photocop-

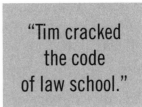

"Tim cracked the code of law school."

ied the test. They were talking about "Ike and Mike", which is a fact situation study. Law professors like to use alliterative names in various case studies. We opened up the exam, and it was the same thing. So...we nailed it...we did very, very well because we went down to Akron and got the test.

There was a guy at law school named Ted Dyke, a labor professor, and he was regular people. He had no airs. He largely had done work with labor unions. He was not particularly well spoken, but he was adorable. We both really liked him. He would teach with a parka on. He didn't wear suits. One day, at the end of the class, he said, "Do youse guys want As in my class?" We said, "Sure we do." He said, "Well, come over to my house. My wife is running for judge. If you stuff envelopes, I'll give you an A." We told him we would be over there after our last class. We got in the car and went to Cleveland Heights where Ted lived with Ann Dyke, who ended up being elected judge. She's still on the bench here at the court of appeals. I told her that story and she said, "*Tim Russert was stuffing my envelopes?*" I said, "You're darn right, he worked on your first campaign." ...and we got As.

This is how law school was for Tim. Tim didn't go to a lot of classes, especially second and third year. But, what law school did for him—it enabled him to study a whole course in two or three or four days and master it and do well. That skill has been with him his whole life. Tim could take what normal students took a whole semester to understand and could do the exact same thing in a couple of days. I was in on those sessions with him, as was Mark Andrews. We would study together. Mark and I went to a lot more classes than Tim did. But, Tim generally was annoyed if he didn't beat me—if he didn't get a better grade. I'd say, "Well, you know, Tim, I went to the classes. Don't you think it's right I should get the better grade?" "No, Marie, I don't. I studied harder."

He did the concert thing. A lot of people have talked about the Bruce Springsteen concerts he did. Tim booked Springsteen in Cleveland when he was in law school. He was friend with the Belkins, who are big music promoters around here. We would go to concerts a lot. We would get in free 'cause Tim would BS his way through. He'd say, "I know Jules Belkin. I've got to see him backstage. These are my colleagues, Colette and Mark."...and we would get in.

> "A lot of people have talked about the Bruce Springsteen concerts he did."

Thursday nights, we'd go down to the Harbor Inn and drink beer. It was just a dive. It's still there—a motorcycle bar. Tim was generous and would always buy the beer. All of us would occasionally get loaded—we all had our moments. But, Tim was so much fun—never reckless or ridiculous—just hilarious.

Tim thought he had cracked the code on how to get through law school. One of the ways we did it was using these Gilbert Study Aids—Cliff's Notes for law students. At the time, they were not particularly well done. They are very well done now. The faculty hated them because instead of reading summaries of cases, they wanted you to read the whole thing. Tim thought that was a horrible waste of time...and it really was.

Gilbert, the guy who started this back sometime in the '70s was Tim's hero. Tim was head of the speakers' bureau in law school, and John Lawson was the student union president. Tim was in town a couple of years ago for the Town Hall Speakers series, and we had a little reception for him. Tim said, "Do you remember I brought the guy in from Gilbert's?" Well, I had forgotten that.

I remember Tim and Lawson went out to the airport and picked him up. I was meeting him at the school. I said, "Welcome to Cleveland Marshall. We're really eager to hear your speech." He looked at me and said, "Nobody has ever asked me to go anywhere." We had made him a celebrity! But the administration went apoplectic that this guy was there on campus.

Tim brought in another guy, Fred Harris. Harris was a big-shot senator from Oklahoma who was running for President of the United States. We took him all over Cleveland one day, driving him everywhere. We had dinner with him. He slept in Tim's apartment (no Shangri-la). That's the only picture I have from law school—Fred Harris and me.

Tim was busy bringing in speakers for law school, booking concerts, going to concerts, going back to Buffalo a lot to tend to his political future—talking to people back there....and hanging out with us.

Tim knew my parents pretty well, too. He thought they were great, and my parents loved him. Every once in a while we'd decide we wanted a decent meal, and we'd go down to my parents' an hour south of Cleveland. Through all the years, he'd tell my Mom, "Well, you made me the best mashed potatoes ever. Those were really good." Every

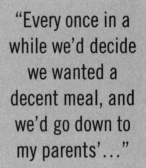

"Every once in a while we'd decide we wanted a decent meal, and we'd go down to my parents'..."

time Mom saw Tim, he said, "Best mashed potatoes of my life, Mrs. Gibbons.".....

Once I was in a snowstorm in Cleveland with Tim for four hours. Tim said that this was the worst day of his life...because he couldn't move. He was a very fast driver and, as much as I liked being driven around by him—because I didn't have a car—he was a scary driver. When he couldn't move, it was like he stopped breathing. He was frustrated beyond words. We were stuck in a snowstorm, and Tim didn't know what to do with himself. But...I had a ball. He was still hilarious in the snow storm....

I was sitting on the stage at a big function a few years ago with Tim, waiting to introduce him. I had this old memory. I said to him, "You know what? You drove me everywhere when we were in school. I didn't have a car." I would get a ride downtown in the morning, but Tim would take me home. Then, if I needed a ride to work, Tim would come back and pick me up and take me to work. If I needed to go home to Canton, he knew before I did that he would take me home. I told him, "That was just so nice. All these kids have their own cars now. If I'd had a car back then, I wouldn't have gotten to hang out with you all the time." He said something silly like he always liked chauffeuring me around to my appointments. He was just a sweetheart.

> "I'd have to admit that I had a crush on him then."

I worked in Florida the summer before I went to law school. I couldn't get a ride to the airport. Tim came and picked me up at six-thirty in the morning to take me to the airport. He was a sweetheart of a person. He made all of us better people because we hung around him. I'd have to admit that I had a crush on him then.

I don't remember Tim ever telling jokes...although he was just hilarious. He didn't have to tell jokes. He would mimic all the law school professors. He had all their cadences down. He would mimic all the leaders in the class who were full of themselves. He had nicknames for everyone. He had almost like a parallel universe of humor regarding everything that was going on in life.

He never quit being the guy we went to school with. He never felt the need to put on any airs. He was still silly and funny and he would call me up and start mimicking a professor from law school...twenty-five years afterward. He still remembered, and they were "on the money" as always.

The phone rang last summer. It was Tim. Tim called me Marie because my name is Marie Colette Gibbons, and the professors would call me Marie even though I am known as Colette. So, for thirty-five years, I've been Marie to him. He says, "Can you get me a ticket to an Indians game on such-and-such a night, six weeks forward?" "Yeah, I can do that." It was the Red Sox and Indians he wanted to see. He said, "There's a fellow, a Veterans Administration physician in San Francisco and you know my wife is from San Francisco. Once when we were out there, my son was sick, and this physician looked at Luke and said he needed to be hospitalized." Tim said that the doctor was a real big baseball fan and that Jacobs Field here is one of the few parks he hadn't been to. Tim arranged for him to go to two Major League parks, put him up for the night, got him tickets on his way to D.C. to visit them. Tim said, "I've done something for him every year because he helped us when my son was sick, and I've never forgotten it." One of my partners from my old firm happens to know baseball, which I don't know. I wasn't going to sit with the guys—I would have been an anchor. I had my friend Bob meet the doctor and then the doctor went on to the next park. But, that was so Tim. Tim paid for everything, and it was something he wanted to do.

> "He had…a parallel universe of humor regarding everything that was going on in life."

I was driving home from work when I heard of his death. I put down the BlackBerry and thought, this has to be a mistake. I went home and watched it all on television. I talked to Mark Andrews and John Lawson. I'd never heard Mark cry like that in all these years. I said, "We have to go to Washington." He said, "I can't. I just can't." He was so devastated. I kept looking for someone to go with 'cause I thought someone at Cleveland State would go. Everybody told me they couldn't go. I got in the car and drove down to Washington by myself even though I was not sure how I would get into the funeral.

One of the things Tim taught me was how to "crash big events," so I left Cleveland with some confidence I would be able to go to Tim's funeral. I was able to get a ticket to the funeral, but I can't tell you how I did it. I gave a blood oath. And there were all these famous people. I'll never be at anything like that again. It was so heartbreaking.

I had a ticket to go the service at the Kennedy Center, but I was too sad. I just went back to the room and watched it on TV and sat there and cried.

> "I was able to get a ticket to the funeral, but I can't tell you how I did it. I gave a blood oath."

On July 11, after Tim died, three of my classmates, Mark Andrews, John Lawson and Neil Robinson, and I went to Lake Chautauqua in southwestern New York state. We drank beer by the lake and we remembered everything we could about Tim. We stayed up until one o'clock in the morning laughing and crying and having a really good time remembering a lot of things. Tim would have approved of our wake for him. Mark and Tim were so close, and Mark was devastated by losing Tim.

Tim was just extraordinary. Maybe with Luke, we'll see his like again, but that is a whole lot of pressure for Luke. Tim adored Luke as I love my son Brian. I'm sure Tim made it clear to him that "to whom much is given, much is expected." But I worry about the pressure on Luke.

One of the things that I think about is that Luke should know what his dad was like in those not-yet-ready-for-prime-time days. While there will be pressure on Luke to ascend to his dad's legacy because he is such a talented and soulful kid, my wish for Luke is that he allow himself a few years of colorful living in graduate school—as his dad did. I think Tim was able to assume so much responsibility at NBC because he had those law school years where there wasn't much we had to do but study and earn a few dollars for some beer. As Luke is famous now in his own right, that may not be possible. But that is my hope for him.

Tim's law school days are a period of his life that does not get too much attention in his sparkling biography. We only had him for three years, but he was a lifelong, devoted, attentive and loving friend to Mark and me. When his biography is written, and there will be many, we want to share his early days, as we all believe those days were critical to the icon he became. Among other things, Tim learned to cut through artifice of professors and a law education system, to read and understand massive amounts of

> "Tim adored Luke as I love my son Brian."

material in two percent of the time it took most people, and to have a really, really good time doing it. My God, he was hilarious.

Marie Colette Gibbons and 1976 presidential candidate Senator Fred Harris.

THE SECRET TO DOING WELL IN SCHOOL? SIT NEXT TO A SMART LEFT-HANDED GUY!

Neil Robinson

Neil Robinson practices law in his hometown of Jamestown, New York, which is seventy miles southeast of Buffalo. He and Russert were law school friends.

T oward the end of law school, Tim cornered me one day and said that I needed to take the bar review course put on by a fellow named Marino. He said it was the best bar review course there ever was and you were guaranteed to pass the New York State bar. I said, "All right," so we signed up for that. At that time, the New York State bar was considerably harder than some of the other state bar exams. I don't know what it's like now. We were quite concerned about it, particularly since we had gone to law school in Ohio, not in New York.

Russert said this was what I had to do: He told me the course was going to be given in a classroom at the University of Buffalo. I signed up for it. I go to the class up there at UB and I walk into this classroom. There's Russert. He knows about fifteen other people. I immediately figured out that he had conned me into signing up for this because if he got enough people, he got it free. It was about three hundred bucks for the course, which, back then, was a lot of money.

What we would do is sit in this classroom for three hours every day, Monday through Friday. There was no live instructor in the classroom—we had to listen to taped lectures for these three hours. Russert had one of those big old reel-to-reel tape recorders he rented or bought cheaply from somebody. It was like something you would borrow from your old uncle. He put it on the desk in front of the room. He would go to the bus station every morning and pick up the tapes of the live lectures from two days before in New York City. We'd sit there and listen to these tapes that were just awful—terrible. We did that for six weeks. Of course, we were scared to death because the New York State bar exam was difficult. The passing rate for it wasn't real high. We sat there every day listening to these tapes. The beauty of all this was that Russert got to keep the tapes. He didn't have to send the tapes back so if you missed one, for some reason, you could arrange a special session where Russert would let you listen to it. Fortunately, we didn't have to pay extra for that.

I rented a room up in the dorm at UB and I was eating Pop Tarts for breakfast and lunch. I didn't have any money for dinner. On Saturday nights, I would buy a quart of beer. The bar exam itself, a two-day event held in late July, was held at the UB law school. Russert said he would wait for me the second day, not to drive, and we would go out after the exam. I'd get a ride over from the dorm, and Russert was living at home.

> "He was wearing his favorite food-covered football jersey and a pair of jeans."

I finished the exam and came outside. There was Russert, waiting for me. He dressed as well back then as he did in later years. He was wearing his favorite food-covered football jersey and a pair of jeans. We hopped in his little Gremlin and *this was a big event!* The first thing we did—we didn't buy regular Rolling Rock or local beer—we bought a 12-pack of Pabst Blue Ribbon. We were driving down Interstate 90 that late afternoon—Russert with a bottle of Pabst Blue in one hand and a steering wheel in the other. Off we headed for the county Democratic picnic. Russert had to go out there and pay his respects.

We went out and spent about an hour there. He said "hi" to all the boys. He was part of the Erie County Democratic process—or machine—if you want to call it that. Joe Crangle, who was head of that, liked Tim....

Then, we went to a bar—I think it's Cole's Bar—up by Delaware Park. It was a Thursday night, and he told me it was "Ladies' Night." We go in there and, of course, none of the ladies wanted to talk to us. We'd been at it for four or five hours. Russert decides he's going to talk to Colette, our very good friend from law school who was back in Ohio. It was about two o'clock in the morning. He goes to this old wooden phone booth at the back of the bar.

> "Tim was screaming into the phone about how we had already finished ours."

We had just finished the bar exam and the Ohio bar exam was the following week, so Colette was still in misery and still having to study for the exam. Tim was screaming into the phone about how we had already finished ours. By that time in the morning, we were perpetually convinced we had passed. We were very happy to be over with it...but we did pass. I remember that we didn't even discuss the exam that night.

That night, Tim and I ended up sleeping at his parents' house. I didn't meet Big Russ, though, because, as I later learned, when I read Tim's book, *Big Russ and Me,* that Big Russ got up *before* one o'clock in the afternoon, which is when Tim and I got up that day. In fact, there was no one in that house when we woke up that afternoon, so, I guess everyone else had things to do. I remember that Tim didn't offer to cook breakfast or lunch for me. We got out of there. Tim drove me back to UB, and I got in my car and drove home.

We took the bar in July. Back then, you didn't hear whether or not you had passed until November. They would send you a letter. I don't know why it took so long—just the torture they put you through. It's been torture ever since with some of the things they make you do in this business.

Russert always had an "in" or an "angle." Before the results came out, I got a phone call one morning in the office where I was a law clerk. It was ten o'clock in the morning, and I picked up the phone to answer it. I remember hearing Jethro Tull blasting through the phone. Russert is screaming, "WE PASSED!" Somehow he found out early and he called to tell me we had passed the bar exam. Tim always knew somebody who knew somebody—that's how Tim Russert operated! God, he was great.

Then you had to go up in December to a "character committee," where they interview you. I was in Buffalo with Tim for that. Tim said we should get something to eat. We went across the street to a restaurant tavern. Tim is talking to some guy at the bar who is doing shots. Tim is talking away with him. Then, Tim came back to where I was and I asked him, "Who was that guy?" He said, "That's the next mayor of Buffalo, Jimmy Griffin." Tim was pretty well tuned in. He knew that Griffin was going to be the mayor.

About three years ago, I was in Buffalo. My daughter was meeting my wife and me there. She was getting tickets for the Syracuse-UB football game on Saturday evening. Somehow, my daughter knew the bartender at Cole's. We go in there. I wasn't thinking much of it. I said, "I think I've been to this place before." I looked around. I said to my wife, "Wonder if there is a wooden phone booth in the back." I walked to the back and, sure enough, there it was....so it had to have been the same place Tim and I went to that night long ago.

Tim always had an unbelievable interest in politics. You know when you were a kid, those people who were interested in politics all the time were nerds. He had that interest...but he wasn't a nerd. He was an awful lot of fun to be around.

After we were sworn in, after we were admitted as lawyers in Rochester, he and I went out and had a couple of drinks and talked for a while. He was in Washington at the time. He told me, "You've got to come down and see me." But I never made it down.

> "Tim always had an unbelievable interest in politics."

Tim was a blast to be with. He never would sit still. In whatever situation we were in, Tim would make it humorous. We never did any more drinking than anybody else did back then, so we never got into trouble—just fun.

Rolling Rock is a beer that was popular in this area of western New York in the middle '70s. When we were in law school and would go out to bars, we would drink the cheapest thing there was, which would generally be draft beer. I don't remember Tim ever tending bar while we were in law school; otherwise, we would have been there—getting a free one!

Shortly after Tim's death, a group of us met at the Hotel Lenhart, which is a 128-year-old Victorian hotel right on the shores of Chautauqua Lake. It was a beautiful place. Chautauqua Institution is there. It's a cultural learning center. Bill Clinton was here, preparing for one of his debates with George Bush when he was running for president. It's a private community and a not-for-profit corporation. People own homes there. It's a vacation and cultural retreat. They have entertainment.

> "Mark Andrews was telling how he had met Tim in the first weeks of law school."

Mark Andrews was telling how he had met Tim in the first weeks of law school. Mark was sitting next to Tim in a class. Mark was called on to answer a question. The professor, as they did in law school back then, humiliated him. They like to do that. Andrews is a tough guy. He was a stevedore on the docks in Ashtabula, Ohio, where he is from. Andrews was going to do his natural thing—he was going to go up and beat the s--- out of the professor. Russert grabbed him and pulled him back and pushed him down in his chair. That's how they met.

About ten years ago, I had to ask Tim a question about something, so I called his office in Washington. His office said he was out of town, but they'd take my name and number. I left my name and number with them. Within forty-five minutes, Tim called me back. I asked him where he was, and he told me that he was in New York City. He was calling me from a limousine. He was self-deprecating about the limousine part. That's the type guy he was.

The Buffalo Braves, an NBA team that's now the Los Angeles Clippers, were in Cleveland playing the Cavaliers, back when the Cavs played in that real rat-hole, Cleveland Arena, on Euclid and 30th. It was a little hockey arena—a real hellhole. Jack Ramsay was the coach of the Braves. Somehow Russert ended up with him. He went out to dinner with him. That's the type of a guy Tim was. He just wasn't afraid of anything.

> "Being brought up in the fifties... everybody... felt a lot more equal than they do now?"

The next day at law school, Tim was telling us all about going out with Ramsay. We told him, "You're full of it." "Oh no. I did." He would charm his way into things.

Being brought up in the '50s—don't you think back then everybody sort of felt a lot more equal than they do now? No matter what your parents did, everybody was sort of in the same boat. I don't think Tim let anything intimidate him. He gave a lot of credit to his father and his parents, and he always seemed to feel secure in what he was doing. And also, in Catholic schools back then, they didn't pamper anyone. In parochial schools, you toed the line. But, by the same token, they instilled self esteem in you.

Cleveland Marshall Law School, of course, wasn't Harvard and it wasn't Yale. There was no snobbishness or elitism there. Everybody came from blue-collar, middle-class backgrounds. Everybody was a little more equal back then. Growing up they were proud of themselves.

A lot of the people in that law school were second-generation Americans. Everybody wanted to get through. Everybody seemed to be pulling together. Some of these other law schools you talk to, the attorneys I work with here in my firm who went to some of the more prestigious Eastern law schools, it was really cut-throat in those schools. The competition. It wasn't that way in our school.

Tim was a natural as far as knowing what he had to know and learning that. Like anything else in life, you learn what you need to learn to do what you need to do.

> "Tim was a natural as far as knowing what he had to know and learning that."

At Chautauqua, there's a tradition of having prominent people lecture there on various subjects. After the celebrity lectures in the morning, they go behind the stage and meet people. My wife and I happened to be sitting up front when Tim was lecturing one time, so we went around back. It just turned out that we were first in line. Tim came out and started talking with us...the line keeps backing up and backing up and backing up. There was no feeling from Tim that "I've got to move you along." It was like he wanted us to stay and talk with him. I finally said, "Tim, we've got to get going. These people are waiting."

Then, I saw him at the law school luncheon they had in his honor about three years ago. Colette was great. She arranged to have us sit right up front. Colette was very close with Tim. He really was an awful nice guy. Even though I hadn't seen him much, I knew that if I needed to talk to Tim, that he would get back to me.

One of my favorite stories that Tim told me: You know how on the garbage truck, the grunts ride on the back. Tim was a grunt. He would stop to get a pizza, and then put the pizza box back there on top of the garbage. He'd ride on the back of the truck and when they'd go by people standing there on the sidewalk or sitting on their porch, Russert would reach in and grab a piece of pizza—like he was getting it out of the garbage—and tell people, "Boy, this stuff is good." Lordy, we're gonna miss him.

Tim would poke fun at people, but he was never malicious or mean or arrogant. Tim was pretty good at mimicking people's mannerisms and their tone of voice. He was in Washington, and he was coming home late one Saturday night or early Sunday morning from some place. He was walking down the street, and the presidential motorcade stopped right in front of him. This was when he was an aide to Moynihan. The limousine door opens up, and Jimmy Carter walks out and bumps right into him and grabs his hand. Later on, in relating the story, Tim imitated President Carter perfectly, "The President said, 'Come worship with me.'" This happened right in front of Carter's church and he was going into the church service. Tim had me in hysterics the way he was telling that story. 'Course they couldn't do that now. They'd have to sweep the sidewalks before they'd let the President out.

One final thing about those "tape" sessions. A guy I know said, "The more I think about that bar exam prep tapes class at the University of Buffalo, it wouldn't surprise me if that guy Marino in New York City knew nothing about the Buffalo "class". Maybe Russert had a buddy in the New York City class taping it for him and they split the $300 per guy. All I know is, many of us would not have passed the bar without those cheesy tapes."

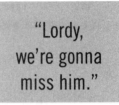
"Lordy, we're gonna miss him."

GILBERT'S STUDY AIDS: THE LAST REFUGE OF SCOUNDRELS

John Lawson

Cleveland attorney John Lawson, a Shaker Heights, Ohio native, has the distinction of once playing on the same pick-up basketball team as Wilt Chamberlain, Bill Russell and Lew Alcindor (Kareem Abdul-Jabbar) at a summer basketball camp. Call it a whim, call it a wild guess, but he probably played guard. After Middlebury College, he was a law school classmate of Tim Russert.

T im's a pretty interesting guy. He knew as early as '75 where he wanted to go. I'm not sure he quite knew what the direct line was that would get him to be so successful. But he knew. He knew he wanted to do legal entertainment.

Tim and I often sat in the back of the same big classes and didn't get very actively engaged in the methods they used at the law school. Tim and I had the same feeling about not letting the law professors intimidate us...which they loved to do.

The class before us had written up a little cheat book we called Filberts. I wrote the second half after we had this one well-known professor. This guy had his own definitions, and once you had those down, you could read anything and it wasn't intimidating anymore. Oh, did Russert love Filberts!

Rolling Rock beer was Pittsburgh, Cleveland, Buffalo. In our junior and senior years, there was the same group of twenty-five guys who would go to the Harbor Inn on Thursday nights. It's a famous old bar down on the flats of Cleveland. We were often part of that crowd. Tim was *always* there and loved Rolling Rock.

I have a little bit of a unique relationship with Tim. I got elected to be the student bar association president for Cleveland Marshall in

'75. Tim and I knew each other from classes, and he immediately came to me. He said, "Look, I've researched this. You've got $50,000 in your budget for a speakers' program. I want to run your speakers' program. I don't want to be one of these lawyers who goes to court. I want to do legal entertainment. I can cut my teeth with this, and it will be perfect. Don't worry. We'll get William Kuntsler." Kuntsler was a famous liberal lawyer at the time. We'd already had Kuntsler there two years before so I knew he'd be able to get him for us.

He wanted to run the speakers' program because it would give him access to that world. We had a little bit of money to play with. We brought in Ramsey Clark and Vincent Bugliosi. Smart move on Tim's part.

The last time I was with Tim was at a Cleveland Marshall cocktail party. He does this little song and dance with me, "Okay, Lawson, what's the greatest speaker we ever pulled off at Cleveland Marshall?" I'm going, "Ramsey Clark? Kuntzler?" Everybody is trying to guess, and there are fifteen or twenty people listening, and finally Tim says, "You and I brought in the president of

"Do not read Gilbert's. It'll warp your analytical mind...."

Gilbert's Study Aids. It was like Christmas for law students. The professors were so angry. They wouldn't talk to us for weeks." Bringing this guy to speak on campus was like inviting Charlie Manson, except Manson would have been more welcome!

Every professor in every class would start off by going, "Do not read Gilbert's. It'll warp your analytical mind. You've got to listen so you will learn how to brief the cases and put down what the rationale is." Everybody would listen to them, and then they'd all use Gilbert's to take the tests. The fact that we brought the Gilbert guy in should say a lot about Tim. It was his idea...I just had to approve of it. I didn't hesitate to approve it...it was at the end of my term. I used student bar association money, and I donated a full set of Gilbert's to the law library at Cleveland Marshall. Russert considered that his greatest coup.

After the guy's speech, it was one of those things where.... I remember one of the property professors walking by and giving us this scowl like a really exaggerated cartoon-type glare. It was one of those things where we knew exactly what he was trying to communicate and he did it well. *You guys are a bunch of ---holes.*

> "He could read the quirkiness of somebody or their mannerisms..."

My theory on Tim Russert being so successful and so well liked? Tim was one of the best imitators ever. He could imitate the professors who were quirky. He could imitate the students who were quirky. That was one of his sophisticated interviewing skills. He could read the quirkiness of somebody or their mannerisms or whatever and give it right back to them. That's a pretty good interviewing skill. It makes the interviewee comfortable. You're not disrupting him by blatantly imitating him like on *Saturday Night Live*. But it's a very subtle skill. Tim was actually quite sophisticated at it.

A lot of our relationship involved business with the speakers' bureau. We started hosting cocktail parties, too. I talked to somebody from one of the bar associations to bring in the booze for us. You need to understand, we were probably the first class after Watergate, so we were a pretty irreverent group. It just was that type of time. The President had resigned. The war wasn't over. We weren't ready to take much of the traditional type of law school. Russert considered the free booze my greatest coup.

After law school, we all knew Tim was with Moynihan. Around 2000 or so, as much as I'd never imagined it, they put me back on the Cleveland Marshall Alumni Board. We weren't a class that was very respectful of the law school. The Ohio legislature had passed the Sunshine Law, and the first thing I did was demand to be in on all the faculty meetings. I bet if you could ask Russert, he would say the same thing. I think he hated law school as much as

I did. When I got put on the Cleveland Marshall Alumni Board, I got put on this committee that picks alumni to be honored every year. Around 2000, I said, "It's time to honor Russert." Every year, they would hem and haw and would finally say, "Get ahold of him." I'd check it out, and it was always too late 'cause he was always booked way in advance and would be speaking at all kinds of graduations, which are in May, as well. Finally, I was able to do it early in the year. I knew that his book was coming out, so I said, "This is the year. If you give me enough leeway to get him lined up, we'll have him come in when his book is released, and I'll line up an autograph thing at the local bookstore, Joseph-Beth Book Sellers, over at Legacy Village," which is a beautiful upscale shopping center in eastern Cleveland.

> Around 2000, I said, "It's time to honor Russert."

Former Cleveland Browns defensive star and current judge Dick Ambrose was the chairman of the committee that year. He said to me, "If you can pull this off, we're with you. It would be great to bring Tim Russert in. It'll bring a lot of recognition to the law school and we'll probably sell a lot of tickets."

I have a friend at Joseph-Beth Book Sellers, Richard Gildenmeister, who is famous in Cleveland. He's been selling books for fifty years. I called him up and said, "Can we get Russert on a book signing agenda for the same day at your store?" So Tim came in, was honored by Cleveland Marshall, and then that night we got him out at Legacy. We got off the dais after Tim spoke at Marshall and he got mobbed by his classmates. Finally somebody, probably Gildenmeister, said, "You've got to get him down to where there are only a couple of hundred people waiting for autographs." I told Tim we had to go. I grabbed Russert and was trying to avoid the crowds. These two women were chasing after us, yelling, "John. Tim. John. Tim." I turned around and Russert says, "Who are these two women?" I said, "Well, one of them is Judge Leslie Brooks Well. She's a federal judge, and the other is Judge Nancy Fuerst." They had pens in one hand and his book in the other hand. Russert said, "I think I'm going to like this." He stopped and he signed their books and then we took him down to the table. Legacy was great. They must have had eight hundred people in line when we got there....

It was the Friday before Father's Day weekend when I heard about Tim's death. I was on the phone with some terrible case I was dealing with. My sister called me on my cell phone and left me a message. It was her first day off from her guidance counselor job at some school in Maine, so she was home watching the soaps for the first time all year. The notice of Tim's death came on the TV. I immediately called Colette, and Neil—two of my very favorite law school buddies. I was trying to get out of town for my daughter's graduation, and I must have gotten fifty phone calls in forty-five minutes. It was just one of those things. The local FOX TV station tracked me down and did an interview with me. When I got back from the graduation on Monday night, I had all these calls, "Nice going, being able to put FOX down like you did."

"I was just trying to say something positive about my friend."

I had found out Tim died. I'm trying to leave town. All of a sudden, Channel 19 is sticking a microphone at me. I said, "What do you mean? I didn't say anything." They all said, "You absolutely did. At the end of your interview, you said, 'And the national media should use Tim Russert as a good example of how to do objective news reports.'" Everybody thought I was cracking on FOX, but it wasn't really my intention. I was just trying to say something positive about my friend.

I think that when Tim Russert died, he was the most trusted person in Washington. I'm going to go out on a limb and say, "I can't name one person who was more trusted, either an elected official or the head of a corporation." I had women who didn't even know him who said they cried all weekend when they found out he died. He was like the guy next door. He didn't look like he should be on TV. He was a little too pudgy. He didn't have a Hollywood face. And, he was honest!

I'll bet you can't guess who Tim Russert's presidential candidate was in '76? Senator Fred Harris from Oklahoma. After law school, Russert called me and said, "You've got to meet me at the Bond Court Hotel tomorrow morning, nine-thirty, room so and so." I go down there, and I knock on the door. Some lady in a bathrobe answers. I 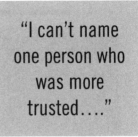 said "I'm looking for Tim Russert." She opens the door. There's Russert in blue jeans with his breakfast on his shirt. Fred Harris is sitting on the bed talking to Tim. I got to meet Fred. Fred actually stayed in touch with him more than any other presidential candidate he ever met. So, that was Tim's candidate.

I probably voted for Harris in that primary. By 1979, I'd already become a Cleveland councilman, at thirty years of age, and got to meet Jimmy Carter. I won the day Dennis Kucinich lost.

LIVING WITH RUSSERT WAS LIKE PLAYIN' HOOKY FROM LIFE

Mark Andrews

Mark Andrews is a towering figure among Ohio attorneys. From his office in Ashtabula, he recently reminisced about his law school days when Tim Russert was his roommate.

Tim Russert was compassionate toward other people. He mixed with everybody. Everybody liked him. I was fortunate to know Tim for thirty-five years and I consider him to be a good friend...but Tim had hundreds of "good friends."

Once you made contact with Tim, it was friendship for life. He was a pretty great guy. The natural intelligence this man had—I guess you could call it "street smarts"—was second to none. He was an intellect when it came to his education, but the guy was so naturally intelligent. He was practical to the point where he could do anything.

Tim could have been president of the United States but for the fact that he liked the job with NBC a lot more than anything else he could aspire to. He knows politics—he lived and breathed politics even back in the days we went to law school. That was his shtick.

Tim and I lived together for two years in law school, and he would read five newspapers every day. I'm not talking about just skimming the papers...he would absorb everything like a sponge. He knew more about politics, and, of course, that's where he worked when we weren't going to law school and right after that. He was a natural. Yet, he never lost touch with the people he met and things that were important in life.

The summer before my first year of law school, I worked at a place called the Union Dock as a stevedore. I was a gripper, and we were moving railroad cars to load them. A few months later, I was sitting in class with Russert and didn't know him at the time. He sat right next to me, and one of the professors was giving me a real hard time. My dockworker passion, I guess, gave rise. I was going to get up out of my seat and go "talk" to this guy. I was so upset. Tim pulled me down by the arm and said, "No, I don't think that's a good thing to do." We became fast friends after that. That happened in the second week of class.

Harvey Leiser was the professor in Torts. He would ridicule the students, and he had me upside down. Some teachers are prone to do this to students. It's part of the Socratic process, where they try to put you under pressure like you would be in a courtroom. They just keep pushing and pushing and pushing. You had to know how to deal with that pressure and the whole technique. They keep asking you questions and you've got to come up with answers. That was the first episode, and it's amazing how much of a fast friend Tim became.

> "…he would absorb everything like a sponge."

Tim was big into music and, of course, he was motivated to trying to make some money. We were always broke. He went to the two big producers in Cleveland, Jules and Mike Belkin. He approached them about having this show with Springsteen, who was not an unknown, who was then an up-and-coming player. The top radio station in Cleveland was WMMS. Disc jockey Kid Leo, who later went to New York City, got in the flow, so to speak, with Tim and the Belkins when they put this on at John Carroll. That was only a 3,000 person venue which was a springboard for Springsteen because then he came back two more times the following year and played at the Allen Theater. That's when he really took off. Tim didn't have anything to do with the latter two appearances, but he ended up getting us great tickets for both of them. He scalped the tickets and used his press pass to get us backstage anyhow.

We first met with Springsteen at John Carroll. We went backstage and met him and Clarence Clemmons. Of course, Kid Leo was there. Our visit was short-lived because the musicians were into their own thing and ready to party into the night. That was very interesting, and one of my favorite memories.

> "We first met with Springsteen at John Carroll."

Tim was gifted. The first couple of years of law school went by, but then in the third year, although he graduated cum laude, he didn't go to that many classes. He was busy figuring out a way to pick his future. He was still heavily connected in Buffalo. That was what enabled him to end up going right from graduation to Moynihan's office a year or so later.

Tim and I were fortunate to get to go to a lot of events, especially after he graduated. We went to the baseball All-Star game in Cleveland. Tim got us into the Commissioner's party. We went to a couple of Super Bowls, including the one in Pasadena when the Buffalo Bills got slaughtered by the Cowboys. We were in San Diego one year and, although, Tim didn't go to the game, he hooked a bunch of guys from Ashtabula up with tickets to go to that game. We went to at least two more. Between Tim and my brother, both of whom had a connection with Chris Berman at ESPN, we went to six Super Bowl games in a period of ten years. We saw a lot of sports events and concerts, which he liked. Tim was quite a guy. Tim liked to take *Meet the Press* on the road to the venue where the big sports event was. He recently did that in Cleveland for the NBA All-Star game. Smart.

UPON FURTHER REVIEW

Tim came into my life in my senior year of law school. He should have been a year behind me, but he was actually two years behind me, because after graduating college, he spent a year working back home in Buffalo before starting law school. Then I went to work for the Cleveland law department as an assistant law director after school. Russert worked there for a year with me part-time during his second year of law school. He tells me I got him his job so I say, "If you want to give me credit, I'll take it." That was a long time ago, but Tim was a good worker. We had a lot of fun.

A number of my family went to Notre Dame so I've been a Notre Dame fan all my life...and still am. In 2002, there was an e-mail that came around from one of my buddies after Tim's address that year to the Notre Dame student body. Plus, Tim received an honorary degree from Notre Dame that day. So, I wrote back to my buddies and said, "You know. It's kind of interesting. The most common remark I remember when I first got to John Carroll was, 'Oh, so you didn't get into Notre Dame either,' and now they're giving us doctorate degrees."

One time I was in my office when Tim came in and said, "Mac, you're not going to believe this." We had a judge who was known for enjoying a liquid lunch. Tim was up there one day in housing court. This judge is on the bench, and he's reading off the violations, "What's this dog feck-ess (feces) in the yard?" Tim was just in stitches telling this story...imitating the judge's drunken voice. Tim was a person who had a zest for life.

All the things we're hearing about Tim are so true. I noticed a lot of stories on TV where people would talk about Tim coming to visit or doing other nice things. Right around the time he graduated from law school, he was going back to Buffalo, so I invited him over to dinner. Tim came over, and we had a wonderful evening. Here's a guy about twenty-three years old, but he brought a little something for my son. When these people talk about those thoughtful things that Tim did, I just think, "Some things never change." His roots were deep and his feelings were genuine. These basic values just came natural to Tim—being considerate and thoughtful. That was just the way he was.

Let me tell you something—Tim was not Mother Teresa...but he was a good guy. He was a guy who knew his roots and never forgot where he came from.

One thing I really feel bad about is that I didn't stay in contact with him as much as I wanted to. If he would come into town, I would always try and go see him. As the years went along, there were fewer and fewer moments when he was in town. There were times when he would come in and we'd go out to have a beer together and spend a couple of hours together. But in his later years, he was doing his books and his work, and we might only get a few minutes with him.

When you went with Tim, he always picked up where we left off. There were no airs about him. He was just a genuine guy. One time I went out with him, we were drinking, and I made a move, hit the table and spilled beer all over his sport coat and his pants. The next thing I know, I get a dry cleaners' bill from him. He was only kidding, but that's Tim. If you called him up, he would always call you back. And, you got him directly.

I was in my office when I got a phone call about Tim's death. At first, you don't believe it. Then, you're stunned. It was such a hard thing to believe. Then, after a while, it was obviously true.

—JIM MACKEY, 60, Cleveland

Chapter 4

The Write Stuff

A Hard Way to Make an Easy Living

HIS FUTURE IS HISTORY

Richard Stengel

Richard Stengel is the Managing Editor of Time *magazine. Stengel, 53, played for Princeton when the Tigers won the 1977 NIT Basketball Championship. Following in the footsteps of another Princeton grad, Bill Bradley, '65, Stengel became a Rhodes Scholar and later a speechwriter for Bradley.*

In 1985, Stengel wrote a remarkable story on a then thirty-four-year-old Tim Russert for Rolling Stone *magazine. Stengel was only thirty at the time. The article was a behind-the-scenes look at NBC's fast rising young executive. The majority of Russert's fans know him for his television work, but Stengel's report showed that Russert had attained amazing status within NBC management.*

Through the wonderful courtesy and cooperation of Richard Stengel and Rolling Stone, *the following is an excerpt from his story.*

He was Moynihan's number-one aide. Then he made Cuomo a household word. Now he's NBC News' youngest vice-president. Nobody, it seems, doesn't need Timothy Russert...

The vanilla ice cream next to the poached pear had mostly melted when Tom Brokaw gently clinked his glass. Smiling, he rose, and the three tables of six in the intimate, darkly wallpapered dining room of the Brokaws' Park Avenue duplex turned to listen to the familiar voice. The dinner was in honor of Brokaw's friend and colleague, Timothy J. Russert, the newest and youngest vice-president of NBC News. At thirty-four, Russert—who resembles the puckish, chubby altar boy that he in fact was—had spent the past two years as counselor to Governor Mario Cuomo of New York and several years before that as chief of staff for Senator Daniel Patrick Moynihan, all the while building a nearly legendary reputation as a street-smart, media-wise political operative. Apart from the guest of honor and his wife, Maureen Orth, who had recently resigned as an NBC correspondent, the guests included NBC News president Lawrence Grossman; Al Hunt, the Washington bureau chief of *The Wall Street Journal*, and his wife, the television correspondent Judy Woodruff; Jim Hoge, the publisher of the *Daily News*; Ken Auletta, the *New Yorker* writer; and the sprightly Mrs. Daniel Patrick Moynihan, whose husband was due to arrive shortly.

The occasion was low-key and unpretentious, but that did not make it any less a ceremony, a kind of laying-on of hands. In a tone both jocular and welcoming, Brokaw said that they were gathered there to celebrate the removal of Tim Russert, a veteran of the Moynihan-Cuomo workfare program, from the public trough. All raised their wineglasses, except Russert, who did not, partly out of modesty, partly because he was drinking beer. The subsequent toasts also had a warmly chafing spirit, but the one that resonated the most in Russert's mind was Ken Auletta's. Auletta, who has written extensively about Governor Cuomo, said that for a public official there was a very fine line between protecting one's political interests and dealing fairly and openly with the media. No one, Auletta said, navigated that line more skillfully than Tim Russert.

> "No one... navigated that line more skillfully than Tim Russert."

But, now, Tim Russert had crossed that line. The hearty, canny, consummate insider from Buffalo who masterminded Moynihan's smashing reelection victory in 1982, the political Sancho Panza with the golden Rolodex who helped catapult Mario Cuomo from a local arena onto the national stage, had gone over to the other side. At NBC, the image maker so adept at manipulating the media from the outside would now be shaping it from the inside. These days, such a crossover is not exactly heretical. The fraternity of political émigrés in televisionland is select, but growing. Bill Moyers worked for President Johnson; Pierre Salinger was press secretary for President Kennedy; Diane Sawyer was a flack for President Nixon; and the man who may well be Russert's prototype, ABC News vice-president David Burke, was the chief of staff for New York's Hugh Carey. The fine line between politics and the media is not so much a real boundary as a sleepy border station lacking guards to check anyone's papers or credentials.

Tim Russert has always been in the business of communication. His wife calls him an infomaniac. The son of a *Buffalo Evening News* truck driver, Russert is never without a bundle of newspapers under his arm. He lugs them on and off trains, taxis, buses. If he is flying from New York to Phoenix and the plane stops in Columbus, he will dash off to buy *The Columbus Dispatch*. He pores over local papers as a doctor takes a patient's pulse: to check the health of the body politic. He was, for both Moynihan and Cuomo, their principal press spokesman, the architect and custodian of their images. For dozens of reporters and columnists, he became an essential stop on the road to a story. Knowing Russert was a prerequisite for anyone in the know; if he had been any more plugged in, he would have been electrocuted. Inevitably described as shrewd, he was the opposite of slick. Among journalists and media people, there is a veritable Russert fan club, composed of members of every political stripe. Liberal columnist Mary McGrory: "He's the best I've ever seen." Conservative columnist George Will: "He is a superb professional, who understands the Democratic party beyond the Washington Beltway, where most of it—thank God for small favors—lives." Democratic political consultant David Garth: "He's the best guy at working the press I've ever encountered." Republican political consultant Roger Stone: "He's the best strategist in the Democratic party."

> "His wife calls him an infomaniac."

Russert was that anomalous thing in politics, the loyal aide who understood the know-how and the know-why, the behind-the-scenes fixer who could work the phones and tell a Madison Avenue sharpie how to craft a thirty-second spot. Part fan, part handholder, part psychologist, part lawyer, part legislator, part speechwriter, part lobbyist, he simply made himself indispensable. And visible. Russert attached himself to bigger men, and then grew under their patronage. "I believe in people who believe in things," he says spiritedly. Not only was Russert instrumental in landing the keynote-speaker assignment at the Democratic convention for Cuomo, he also helped focus the governor's stirring speech. Cuomo is his own best phrasemaker, but Russert got Cuomo to emphasize that graphic image of the Two Cities. He made liberal good intention marketable again. When Gary Hart cried in the middle of the primaries, "Give me a Russert," he became a part of speech: **russert** (rus' . ert) n: a skilled political operative adept at framing and communicating a politician's message while enhancing and expanding his reputation and popularity. NBC can use a russert.

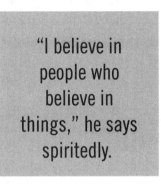

"I believe in people who believe in things," he says spiritedly.

If NBC News were a candidate, it would be the perennial also-ran, the tired campaigner the public has all but forgotten. As the news organization that seems to have a lock on third place in the ratings, the only network that is unable to come up with a successful magazine show, the one news organization that has not been "hot" any time during the past decade. NBC could do with some gussying up. For the past eight years, Russert has spent part of every day thinking how to make television work for him; now he will be working for it. In part, Russert has left his first love for money. At NBC he is making about double the $75,000 he earned with Cuomo. Recently married, he teasingly affirms that he and Orth want "to enlarge the family of New York" (she is now pregnant). The switch, though, was serendipitous—when Larry Grossman offered him the job, it was a move he hadn't really contemplated. Afraid of becoming a political vagabond, Russert was also lured by television's uncanny power of molding the images and ideas that millions regard as reality. "I didn't understand television as well as I wanted. And I wanted to master it." At

NBC, Russert is now helping shape the images that shape the nation.

In Buffalo, says Russert, "you were born a Democrat and baptized a Catholic." In that order. His apprenticeship in the rough and tumble world of ward politics began in 1960 when, at the age of ten, he lost a scuffle with the kid down the block who had ripped down the Kennedy sign from in front of the Russert residence. It was his first political lesson: stay out of a fight you can't win. Crafty Timmy then persuaded a paperboy chum to let him deliver part of the boy's *Evening News* route, and Russert slipped Kennedy brochures into the fold before flinging the paper onto neighborhood doorsteps.

In school, he was a little dynamo, and the nuns doted on him. He was a do-gooder who didn't really seem to be a goody-goody. From the first, he says, "I don't know what motivated me more, fear of failure or the need for success." Named, in 1968, the Outstanding Youth of the Year of the Diocese of Buffalo, he chose a small and undistinguished Jesuit school in Cleveland, John Carroll University. Not only did he become president of the student body, he was the campus impresario, booking and organizing rock concerts. "I learned an awful lot about dealing with temperamental talent and egos," he says with a laugh and a roll of the eye. "Politics is the same thing."

> "He was a do-gooder who didn't really seem to be a goody-goody."

The college graduate went to work for the city comptroller of Buffalo, George D. O'Connell, and learned ward politics at the feet of Frank Szuniewicz Jr. ("Frankie Son-of-a-Bitch," he called himself), the leader of the fifteenth ward of Buffalo. Szuniewicz took him to the Roosevelt restaurant every day for lunch, where Russert wolfed down beef-on-kümmelweck sandwiches and the savory anecdotes of political old-timers. "Timmy learned street politics," remembers Szuniewicz, "which is just finding out what people think down the street, not what's written in the news-paper." Russert knew that he could make it in Buffalo, but that Buffalo would not make it for him. Law was the answer, and he enrolled at the Cleveland Marshall College of Law, a middling law school back in Ohio. Law school did not give him a profession so much as a technique for problem solving.

"Moynihan... saw in Russert a younger self."

After graduating, Russert was working in Buffalo as the western regional representative for Sena-tor Daniel Patrick Moynihan when the great blizzard of 1977 descended. As the snow fell, he rose to the occa-sion—organizing relief, then unwinding at what he describes as "the best parties in the history of the city." Three days later Moynihan arrived to tour the area. There he found Russert, in an oversize parka and Timberland boots, the young wizard of the bliz-zard. "You're coming back with me," Moynihan said, "And," recalls Russert, "I got on the plane, no suitcase, nothing."

Together they drafted a letter to President Carter asking for disas-ter aid. Once in Washington Moynihan urged him to stay. It didn't take much persuading. Moynihan had a crack staff—Ivy League degrees and a certain intellectual arrogance. Russert, the truck driver's son from the sticks, was a bit cowed. "I didn't rec-ognize, for example, some of the references to Trotskyites and Mensheviks, or liberalism in the CCNY cafeteria." But he soon realized that he did know a thing or two that they didn't know. "I understood what a Democratic senator from New York needed to stand for," says Russert. "And I enjoyed saying sometimes, 'That's an interesting idea, sir, but it won't play in Buffalo.'"

Moynihan, the child of Hell's Kitchen who had made it in the Establishment, saw in Russert a younger self. At twenty-nine, after two and a half years as a legislative assistant, the energetic and high-spirited lawyer who operated the telephone like an extra appendage became the youngest chief of staff in the U.S. Senate. He remained Moynihan's principal spokesperson and a favorite of the press. He drank with journalists, gossiped with them, knew what they needed for a story and how to get it. When a reporter was desperate to reach a source, Russert would pluck the magic number from his spinning wheel of names. "Look, here it is," he would say. "If he asks you where you got it, say it was in the files. So put it in your files, take it out, and call him." The Jesuits would be proud.

"The Jesuits would be proud."

With Moynihan facing a potentially difficult reelection fight in 1982, Russert took a leave of absence as chief of staff to become campaign manager. "If you were writing a military history," explains Moynihan, "Tim would be among those commanders who are brilliant at forcing their antagonists into untenable positions by exerting pressures that they don't entirely recognize at the time." Commander Russert's most memorable maneuver was the Caputo Gambit. Russert anticipated that Congressman Bruce Caputo would be Moynihan's strongest Republican challenger. He prepared for battle by reading every Caputo clip he could find, assiduously marking down each vote, fact, and assertion on yellow legal pads. "Inconsistencies began to emerge," says Russert. What materialized was Caputo's contradictory claim about a military career. Russert mentioned this discrepancy to two journalists who were to have lunch with Caputo. The first thing out of Caputo's mouth after he opened his napkin was that he had served in Vietnam. The reporters checked it out. It was false. Caputo was kaput. Moynihan went on to win with the largest majority in a midterm election in the history of the Senate.

That same November a plucky lawyer from Queens named Mario Cuomo was elected governor of New York. With Moynihan's blessing, and Mrs. Moynihan's observation that "everybody has to grow up and leave home," Russert went to work for the new governor. He was drawn to him by the question that Cuomo himself seemed to personify: Can government be effective and efficient and still be progressive and compassionate? Officially, Russert was Counselor to the Governor, a title concocted by Cuomo that barely suggested the myriad ways that Russert served him. Russert participated in the formulation of policy and legislation, ran the press office and was Cuomo's principal spokesman. Russert was all things to Cuomo, but not to every reporter. Some local journalists, muttering that Russert only shmoozed with national types and TV reporters, grumbled that Russert was better at swapping stories than pushing papers.

In the jargon of television, Cuomo might be described as a "high concept" politician. Russert honed that concept. "Tim is excellent at synthesizing things and then articulating them," says Cuomo. That is precisely what he helped the governor do at the Democratic convention in San Francisco. "He was able to help me make my case in a way that I could not have done by myself," says Cuomo. Russert was credited with giving him so-called national exposure. Much of that consisted of orchestrating television coverage and organizing Meet Mario breakfasts for VIPs the governor might not have met otherwise. "Tim has great credibility," says Cuomo generously, "and I borrowed some of that credibility."

But NBC wanted to borrow it also. Not long after Larry Grossman was named NBC News president, his friend, the Washington lawyer and former Nixon White House counsel, Leonard Garment, suggested Grossman look up Russert. Give him a call, Garment told his chum, he's an Irish *mensch*. The rabbinical-looking Grossman and the

> "Tim is excellent at synthesizing things and then articulating them..."

boyish, bearish Irishman hit it off. "They have one big thing in common," says Garment, "they both have *fun* while succeeding." Grossman called Cuomo to make him an offer for his valued counselor. Cuomo, realizing he could not stand in the way of such an opportunity, reluctantly said okay.

The fifth-floor executive offices at NBC News are a study in muted power: beige carpeting, beige walls, beige desks, beige executives. Russert's expansive office is situated next to Grossman's—prime real estate in the geography of office politics. Grossman is the fifth president of NBC News in eleven years. The thoughtful, bearded savior of PBS, Grossman is an advertising man by profession. Like Russert, Grossman was never a newsman. But Grossman knows that television is not a vocation of long apprenticeships; a tyro like Russert can adapt quickly.

> "No one seemed overly concerned about possible political bias."

Even among NBC veterans, there were few raised eyebrows when a news neophyte like Russert came aboard. The general view was that his lack of journalistic credentials was balanced by his experience in the political arena. No one seemed overly concerned about possible political bias. Grossman acknowledges that after hiring Russert the first question he was asked by the NBC board of directors was whether the new vice-president would be partisan, but he finds the whole issue tedious. "Look, we're all grown-ups here," Grossman says wearily. Russert's counterpart at ABC, David Burke, suggests there is a built-in safeguard against bias. "News people are the most cynical in the world," says Burke, "and they will double-think anyone's motives. Their very skepticism is one guarantee that people who have crossed the line will be held to a tough standard."

Crossing the line, though, may well be the wrong metaphor. Actually, the connection between politics and the media is incestuous, so intertwined that it is hard to separate one from the other. Such coziness seems to bother almost no one. And "why should it?" asks George Will. "What I think is supposed to be at jeopardy here," says Will, "is the moral purity of the media. But you have to believe in that first. I can believe many things—six impossible things before breakfast, Lewis Carroll wrote. That I can't believe."

Little more than two months after joining NBC, Russert is worried less about purity than about numbers. He is charged up by the fact that NBC News has been in second place, behind CBS, for three straight weeks. The network's new theme, NBC NEWS ON THE MOVE, is his anthem as well. Along with Grossman, he is determined to return NBC to the glory days of Huntley and Brinkley, when theirs was *the* news to watch.

Russert's commitment to that task begins before sunup.

6:30 a.m. His alarm goes off, and he groggily watches the tail end of NBC's early-morning news program, *NBC News at Sunrise*. Leaving his brownstone apartment on Manhattan's Upper West Side, he buys the three New York papers. During the twenty-minute cab ride to the Cardio-Fitness Center at Rockefeller Center, he reads as much as he can. A believer in recycling information, he asks the driver, "You want these papers?" The cabby looks at him as if he were trashing the backseat. Russert takes them.

8:30 a.m. The Cardio-Fitness Center: Clad in the required uniform—a pale-blue T-shirt and navy-blue shorts—Russert is doggedly pedaling an Air-Dyne stationary bicycle while watching Jane Pauley wind up on the *Today* show on a television screen above him. After the workout, he walks across the street to NBC and stops by the *Today* set to chat with the show's producer, Steve Friedman. Friedman laughs when Russert tells him that the guys at Cardio-Fitness pedaled faster during the show's rock & roll segment on Little Richard.

9:15 a.m. Grapefruit juice, no coffee. He scans *The Washington Post*, *The Wall Street Journal* and *USA Today*. His office is orderly now, but by 5 p.m. is will resemble a battlefield strewn with crumpled newspapers, the casualties of the day's events. He stops by Grossman's office to discuss strategy for an upcoming affiliates' meeting.

9:45 a.m. The first meeting of the day in a day full of meetings. In the medium of television, meetings are the method. With styrofoam cups of coffee steaming before them, eight NBC News vice-presidents, the executive producers of *Nightly News*, *Today* and *Sunrise*, sit in Breuer chairs around a long, rectangular table in room 508. At the head sits Grossman, wearing what appears to be a varsity-letterman's sweater with the NBC insignia embla-zoned on it, making him look like chief cheerleader. Joe Bartelme, the general manager for U.S. news, and Jerry Lamprecht, the gen-eral manager for foreign news, run down the day's stories. Grossman rubs his beard. "Anything else?" he asks. The meeting is brief, fifteen minutes, and terse. On the way back to their offices, Russert and Grossman discuss a correspondent who has been doing an impressive job. "He's a strong writer, very poetic, and an avuncular presence on the screen," Russert says. Grossman nods.

10:45 a.m. Russert meets with an advertising executive about promotional ads. He finds them self-serving and tells the fellow to have the copy rewritten. At the moment, Russert's principal chore is to be the point man in NBC's aggressive effort to inte-grate and promote the news organization. "The idea is that news should get a fair share of what in effect is internal promotion," says Russert, "with each individual show, *Nightly News*, *Today*, *Sunrise*, feeding the others." Russert evaluates every on-air promotion and is the prime mover in the NBC NEWS ON THE MOVE campaign. One part of the plan calls for NBC entertain-ment stars, like the Great Communicator Bill Cosby, to tout NBC News in brief spots. "Isn't it just as important to see someone talking about NBC News as a ten-second promo for *Punky Brewster*?" says Russert. "It's just like politics. You institutionalize an image and people come to believe in it."

12 noon. The editorial board meeting. Clustered about a round table at the north end of Grossman's office are executive vice-president Tom Pettit, senior vice-president John Lane, Brokaw, John Chancellor, NBC's *eminence grise*, Grossman and Russert. Instituted by Grossman, the board is a kind of collective corpo-rate conscience cum big-boy bull session. They examine the merits of current issues and stories and look ahead to future ones. Brokaw, anchorman of the *Nightly News*, values Russert's presence for a number of reasons. "I feel like he's someone I went to high school with," says Brokaw. "But, more than that, Tim is someone who can come in my office, look me in the eye and tell me something I may not want to hear."

3:30 p.m. The *Nightly News* scheduling meeting on the fifth floor. The news producers discuss that evening's lineup of stories. Russert attends this meeting in order to keep abreast of what's happening. He mostly listens, injecting the occasional wisecrack. "It's important for news executives to respect the integrity of the producers and their show," he says. "You can't just say, 'I think you should lead with such-and-such a segment.' They would throw you out the door. As they should." Afterward Russert meets with a corporate honcho to discuss the contracts of various on-air talent and review some of NBC's efforts to stay out of the ratings cellar. "Ratings are what this business is all about— being there first," he says, clenching his fist. For Russert, the uncompetitive life is not worth living.

5:45 p.m. The vice-presidents gather once again. "We rehash the day, find out what's on people's minds and talk about upcoming stories," Russert says. When the meeting breaks up, Russert vainly attempts to answer a stack of messages. At 6:15 p.m., as he is on his way out the door, the phone rings. His secretary has gone, so he picks it up himself. "Mis-ter Chan-cel-lor," he says, spreading out the syllables in comradely salutation. He listens, shifting his weight from one foot to the other. "I agree. Let's talk after the show."

6:30 p.m. Russert, Lane and Pettit wander by Grossman's office to watch the first network feed. If they are dissatisfied with the show, it can be revised for the 7 p.m. broadcast. Several months ago, after the unexplained crash of an American plane in Central America, a report came over the wire that Barry Goldwater, the chairman of the Senate intelligence committee, was making an announcement at 6:30 p.m. The clarification would be too late for the first feed. "I knew that if the chairman was briefed," recalls Russert, "the vice-chairman was also briefed. The vice-chairman happened to be Daniel Patrick Moynihan." Russert rang Moynihan and garnered enough declassified details to enable NBC to lead with the story. After the show, Russert's evening may be devoted to a dinner party, or perhaps a different passion: movies. On a rainy Sunday, he might see three films. And, on the off chance that a rerun of *Cool Hand Luke* is on television, he will watch that, as he has already, *eleven* times before.

11:30 p.m. At home, Russert's nightly dilemma: What to watch? What to watch? Carson? *Nightline*? Or his beloved *Honeymooners*? Switching channels just wasn't the answer. Technology rescued him from his nightly quandary. Last December he had three television monitors installed in the living room. He ends the day as he begins it, bathed in the glowing light of a television screen.

Television news has replaced politics at the center of Russert's life and imagination. He already seems to regard his new field with the same veneration he had for his old one. Russert confutes the stereotype of the detached network executive insulated in the steel-and-glass cocoons of Sixth Avenue. He is a populist in the world's most popular medium. For him, popularity is not synonymous with inferiority: "The public is not beguiled." He mulls this over. When he concentrates, he leans forward in his chair, hunched over, legs spread, like a high-school coach diagramming a play in the dirt. "They know what they want, and what they want is usually right. I really believe, for example, that the better candidate wins." Russert is a democrat with a small *d*. Perhaps that is why he takes so much ribbing from his former boss about joining the glossy world of network television. According to Governor Cuomo, a stand-up comedian *manqué*

"There are just two things Tim has to do: get his weight under control, and never, never, lacquer his nails."

whose deadpan delivery is flawless, "There are just two things Tim has to do: get his weight under control, and never, never, lacquer his nails."

He doesn't have the time or the inclination to anyway. Nor does he have the temperament to worry about those who may suspect him of having a hidden political agenda. Russert signed a standard, three-year NBC executive contract. It expires in October of 1987, just in time, suggest some old political hands, for Russert to hitch his star to the Cuomo for President bandwagon. "I've always lived with rumors and speculation," he says. "I made a conscious decision to leave politics for the media. I have embarked on a new career. The decision surprised a lot of people. To suggest that this is all part of some Machiavellian scheme is absurd."

> "...To suggest that this is all part of some Machiavellian scheme is absurd."

Ah, but the question is, What would Metternich, not Machiavelli, say about it? Russert is fond of recounting an anecdote about the cunning Austrian statesman. The story is instructive. "Metternich was woken up in the middle of the night," Russert says, with a hint of impish glee, "and told that the Russian ambassador had just dropped dead. Metternich rubbed his eyes and said, 'What could be his motive?'" Russert chuckles. If he has ulterior motives, he is keeping them to himself.

Right now, his allegiance is to NBC and the news. Russert considers his desertion: "In politics, you know what the press is going to ask, you know what they're going to pounce on and how they're going to take what you said and interpret it. Having anticipated that for eight years," he says with a knowing smile, "it's now pretty much the way I thought it was."

The one thing that he feared might happen, didn't. Russert dreaded post-politics decompression. "Politics is the kind of profession that you're making ten decisions per minute; yes, no, yes," he says. "Suddenly, people leave politics, and the phones don't ring." He has discovered that the metabolism rate is just as frenetic in television. "This is the closest thing there is to the day-in, day-out concern in politics about what's going on in the world," he avers, turning up the volume on the center monitor for a report by an NBC correspondent on Capitol Hill. "You don't have a week to think about it," he announces with enthusiasm. "You have to decide what things mean in a few minutes. It really is blood and guts." He grins. "It's wild."

HEAR ME NOW, WATCH ME LATER

Mary Ann Ahern

Mary Ann Ahern is a political reporter for NBC5 News in Chicago. She has reported on many major stories, including Princess Diana's visit to Chicago, several papal trips by Pope John Paul II, and the 2000 and 2004 presidential elections. She graduated with a B.A. from John Carroll University in 1976. She serves on John Carroll's Board of Regents.

While Tim was in law school, he ran or was the bartender at the campus bar at John Carroll University, the Rathskeller. In those days you could drink at eighteen—that lovely 3.2 beer.

Every year in August, my family would have a big party for the College All-Star Football Game in Chicago. All the John Carroll gang would come out to Northeast Indiana, where we lived across the street from Lake Michigan in a big, old, well-worn house. Nobody cared if twenty people were there. Tim would sit and talk and talk to my mother. She would say, "Oh, Mary, that Tim—he's going to run for Congress some day. I know he is."

I work for the NBC station in Chicago as a reporter. On Fridays sometimes I get to sneak out early. On June 13, 2008, I had just finished for the day. My daughter was with me. I could hear someone talking at the news desk. Someone in Washington called our desk and told them about Tim's death before it was announced. I could hear them say something about Russert, so I asked what happened. They said he'd had a fatal heart attack. I said, "No way!" I couldn't believe it. I went back to my desk and sat there and cried out loud. I've never done that—ever. People came over to me and all I could say was, "I'm sorry. He was such a fabulous guy to me. I cannot tell you." It was so awful. I sat there for a while. My daughter was overwhelmed. People offered to take her home if I was going to stay and try to do a story. I said, "No. I honestly want her to stay." She was okay with it, too. She wanted to stay. She'd heard all the stories over the years about Tim Russert.

Whenever Tim would come to town, my brother Marty was the concierge and would get the Chicago crowd together. He could call ten or fifty people in a matter of moments to tell them, "Russert's going to be here. T.J.'s going to be here." They'd all show up. Tim would give a speech at the Economic Club or whatever. He would always want to go see his John Carroll buddies. They'd meet and have a great time with him, whether it was an hour or three. Then he'd scoot off to the airport and be gone.

> "...and, if you had asked him what my first name was, I'm not even sure he could have told you."

I knew Marty would be devastated. He'd just talked with him the week before...on the Friday before, he had called to talk to him. After they talked, Marty would always call me. Tim would often ask, "How's your little sister? How's she doing? Are they treating her all right?" ...and, if you had asked him what my first name was, I'm not even sure he could have told you. I was just "Little Bergy." If I saw him around in other areas, it would always be, "Hey Bergy. How's it going?"

My first TV job was in Peoria. It usually takes two-and-a-half years before you can climb another rung on the ladder. I wanted to move from Peoria to Atlanta. As it gets down to three people for the job at NBC in Atlanta, I called Tim and said, "Please. Can you give them a call?" I think I may have promised Tim my first-born! Tim came through for me. I promised him I wouldn't disappoint him. I was in Atlanta for almost five years covering politics there, including the '88 convention. My goal was to get back to Chicago. The same kind of scenario—it took a year from when I first connected with the Chicago news director to him telling me there was going to be an opening. Once again, I had Russert call for me...as a closer.

When Tim wrote his second book, *Wisdom of Our Fathers*, he came to Chicago and spent the day. Our station followed around with him. Folks in this area showed up and were thrilled. Some of the people had submitted stories that were in the book. Tim remembered everybody. 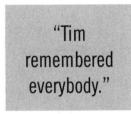 When someone would tell him who they were he'd say, "Oh, you're so and so. Your father was George," or whatever. He knew all their stories. It was incredible.

The long-time political guy, Dick Kay, at my station was retiring that week. I was holding out for a parking spot here at the station. That sounds so crazy! It's the last "sign" of finally having "made it". Not only do you have the job, but you have the free parking. They weren't giving it to me...and they weren't giving it to me! Tim knew this 'cause I had talked to him throughout the afternoon when we were hanging around. We run into the "Big Boss" when he came looking for Tim. I'm walking with Tim to get his cab to go to the next book signing. The Big Boss said, "Oh Tim, how are you? Good to see you. Our political guy has retired." Tim said, "Yeah, and I think this gal, Bergy here, is going to be your next one." He said, "Well, she's driving a hard bargain." Tim played it great. He said, "Bergy, what's the deal? What are you looking for?" I said, "All I need is the parking spot. Just looking for the parking spot." Tim said, "Come on. What are you driving?" "Just a little minivan. No big deal." The poor boss didn't know what to say. He walked away...and then Tim said, "Little Bergy, I think I got you that parking spot." Sure enough, within twenty-four hours, I had a parking spot. And, Tim called later to check on it. He said, "Did you get it or not?" That's the kind of guy Tim was. He loved knowing that was something he helped me on. It was great.

Tim would only come to Chicago to the newsroom maybe once a year. He might be in Chicago, but he had so many friends here that when he came to do a speech or a book signing, he wanted to go see them and talk to them. That was his chance to reconnect. He tried to not hang out too much there unnecessarily if he didn't have to.

When I mentioned in the newsroom early on that I knew Tim Russert, I think some of the people thought I was lying. In fact, our station had arranged a Russert interview with one of our anchors. Russert ended up calling them and saying, "No. I'm not doing it with them. I'm doing it with Little Bergy. I already made a deal. I'm doing it with her." The boss was, "What's the deal?" I said, "I'm sorry. I told you guys I knew him, but you didn't really believe me." He had made a commitment to me.

I'm five years younger than Tim. I never had a crush on him. As a young kid, even then, Russert was a guy who had a command. When he walked into a room, he was bigger than life. Everyone was wowed!

> ...it's great that Brokaw's doing it, but you think, "Where is Tim? Why isn't he back yet?"

My husband, Tom, works for the government and would have to go to Washington periodically, so he would go over to watch *Meet the Press*. It was fun for him to see it live. Tim would come down to see who was sitting in the crowd and would say, "There's my favorite federal agent."

I've been so bummed. You watch TV on Sunday, and it's great that Brokaw's doing it, but you think, "Where is Tim? Why isn't he back yet?"

Tim's untimely death has made me do a lot of thinking about my mortality. Part of me is angry that he worked so hard. I know he loved it and wouldn't have wanted it any other way. But, he worked so hard, and 2008 was such an incredible year. I'm here in Chicago, and we're working hard because of Obama. I've been to several of the primaries, not every single one, but I've been exhausted. I had a week off, and I slept for a week! I was so tired.

These guys worked at an incredible pace. Now, I think, "He's gone. Darn it."

Tim was one of those guys who wouldn't settle for doing anything halfway. He wanted to be the best at what he did. He was student union president at little John Carroll. Even though he went to Cleveland State for law school—yeah, he didn't go to Harvard or Yale—he did fabulous things with his education. Almost to prove to everybody, "Hey, you don't necessarily have to have the Ivy League education."

> "...You can find a million stories about people he touched and helped."

The whole give-back part.... You can find a million stories about people he touched and helped. He would get tickets for people. One kid I saw told how he was engaged at the Nationals Stadium 'cause Tim gave him tickets and arranged it all. That's the "give-back" to other people. That's small stuff, but it's the way of people looking out for each other. That's the kind of guy he was.

WASHINGTON:
FIRST IN WAR, FIRST IN PEACE,
LAST IN THE NATIONAL LEAGUE

Richard Benedetto

Richard Benedetto served as the White House/national political correspondent for USA Today *and as political columnist for Gannett News Service. He reported political news for thirty-five years at the local, state and national levels. His coverage of the administrations of Presidents Ronald Reagan, George H.W. Bush, Bill Clinton, and George W. Bush has been in* USA Today *(of which he is a founding member),* Buffalo (N.Y.) Evening News, *the* Utica (N.Y.) Daily Press *and* Observer-Dispatch *and Gannett News Service. Benedetto has reported on every presidential campaign since 1984. The memoir of his career,* Politicians Are People, Too *was published in 2006.*

I knew Tim Russert since he was a teenager. By a very strange coincidence, I happened to be his next-door neighbor in West Seneca, a suburb of Buffalo. I was working for the *Buffalo Evening News* at the time. Tim was still in high school. His mother, father and three sisters lived next door. His younger sister, Katherine, whom everybody called Kiki, would babysit for my two-year-old daughter. His oldest sister, Betty Ann, called B.A., used to ride down to work with me in the mornings.

Tim was going to Canisius. One of the most vivid memories I have of young Tim at that time was the day of Bobby Kennedy's funeral. Tim had been a volunteer in the Bobby Kennedy presidential campaign in 1968. He was a senior in Canisius High School. He was a big Bobby Kennedy supporter. The funeral was on a Saturday afternoon, and the funeral train from New York City to Washington, D.C. was traveling by. There was television coverage every inch of the way. Tim was sitting in the back yard with his hands locked together. He sat there for the entire time of the train traveling from New York to Washington. He was just crushed by the scene. It set him back.

I kept walking back and forth over there from my house to his house and talking to him. We were just commiserating on what actually happened. It wasn't like I was telling him to cheer up. The cause Tim was fighting for—working for—was the Vietnam War. At that time, Tim was against the war. Kennedy was against the war, so Tim saw him as the guy who could help end it.

Tim, even at a very young age, was politically active and politically smart, which made him stand out to me. He was really up on politics for such a young kid. Tim went on to college and got involved in politics there.

I moved away from Buffalo, but I started crossing paths with Tim again when I was covering state politics and he was working for Senator Moynihan. I covered the first Moynihan campaign in 1976 when Tim was working on the campaign for him. I knew he was working for the campaign, but when we crossed paths, it was a pleasant surprise.

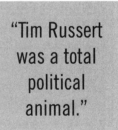

"Tim Russert was a total political animal."

Then, Tim went to work on Moynihan's staff. I was working in Albany for the Gannett News Service at the same time. Tim worked out of Washington, but he would come up to Albany once in a while on business for Senator Moynihan. We would see each other again from time to time along the campaign trail.

Tim Russert was a total political animal. He would fit in no matter where he went. The thing is that being the kind of person who is as versed in politics as Tim was, when he came to Albany, he could discuss politics in Albany and things that affected Albany. When he would go back to Washington, he could discuss the politics of Washington. I'm sure that as a top aide for Senator Moynihan, Tim knew the politics of every city in New York state.

Tim later went to work in Albany, New York, for Mario Cuomo in 1983 when Mario became governor. By that time, I had left Albany and had gone to Washington. I worked for *USA Today*, starting in 1982, the first year of *USA Today*.

> "There hadn't been any track record of any national newspaper working."

I was with Gannett News Service, so when they were putting together a team of people to put the new paper together, I was asked to join it. I was working out of Albany at the time and the deal was that I only had to commit to six months. If *USA Today* didn't fly, your job was guaranteed—you could go back to your old job. But, you had to commit to working there for six months. I commuted from Washington to Albany and back during that period of time. We began working as a start-up team about two months before the paper's introduction. We started putting together prototypes and developing layouts and designs. At the start, I had my doubts that it would work. There hadn't been any track record of any national newspaper working. The night we put the paper to bed, they broke out champagne in the newsroom. I remember standing there with two or three other reporters and saying, "What if this paper comes out tomorrow morning and nobody buys it?"

It only debuted in the Washington area. The next day, there were a lot of different things. It was mainly being talked about on shows like *Today* and *Good Morning, America*. There was plenty of publicity. That next day, the paper sold out in Washington immediately. You couldn't even find a copy. It seemed to succeed. What they did was to roll it out in different cities from week to week—Boston, Minneapolis—all the big market areas. Finally, by the end of the year, it rolled out in every big market.

They sensed fairly early on that the paper was selling. It wasn't until three or four months passed that they began to talk about a permanent staff and moving people to Washington. They then made offers to people to move to Washington to work full time. In

December of '82 I decided to take their offer and stay on there. It was exciting. How many people get a chance to say they've started a newspaper? And, how many people could say they started a newspaper that actually is the biggest selling newspaper in the country? I wrote the very first cover story in the very first edition—it was about suburban sprawl. That was twenty-five years ago and suburban sprawl is still a problem.

I was not working in the area of using all the different colors in different sections and having the graphs and charts. A whole team of people were solely involved with design. Another whole team of people were involved with layout. It was the brainchild of Al Neuharth, the founder of the paper, and he wanted a colorful paper. He said that people were used to television and, therefore, we need to give them a paper that's going to capture their attention and compete with television for their time.

At that time, the newspaper business itself was tied to the old format and thought that you shouldn't make changes. Change comes slow to newspapers. Papers did begin to start using more color. They started using more graphics. They started to loosen up their layout, and started sprucing their stories up. That was how they imitated us, but to think that they could just go to that complete format—I think they just didn't think it would work for them. And maybe it wouldn't have.

A lot of the old newspaper "elite" looked down their noses at *USA Today*...and they still do—to a certain degree.

There were several Buffalonians who stayed in Buffalo, who worked at the *Courier Express*, the morning paper which folded back around the time *USA Today* was just coming out, and who came to work at *USA Today*. One who is still there is Eric Brady, who writes a lot of cover stories in sports. He's close to Tim's age.

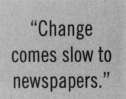

"Change comes slow to newspapers."

I was older than Tim Russett. When I moved to Tim's neighborhood, I was a working adult and Tim was in high school. That neighborhood was a typical working-class neighborhood, single-family homes with detached garages. Most were smaller, three-bedroom homes, single-car garage. People didn't have two cars in those days when the houses were built. Most of the houses were probably built right after the war. The neighborhood had very nice people. Everybody was friendly and got together at backyard parties. In 1969, when the astronauts landed on the moon, Tim's parents had a big party in their yard.

> "...he had an encyclopedic memory that would pull that information right out."

I was working in Albany when I learned Tim was going to Washington. When I would watch *Meet the Press*, I would often say to people, "I can't believe that's that kid from down the street." I would tell people that I knew Tim Russert way back when. I would say, "I know him *before* he was Tim Russert."

In Washington, Tim was around all the time. He was a big presence in Washington because he went everywhere and did everything. He was everywhere from baseball games to parties. He was always around...always a presence. He always would remember something in a personal way about people so that when he would see them, he'd say, "Hey, How's your *uncle I met 20 years ago?*" He had that way about him that he could remember something personal about everybody he would run into. Even though it may have only been one time that they'd had a meeting with Tim, he had an encyclopedic memory that would pull that information right out.

Had Tim Russert ever been a politician, he'd have been a great one. He had that ability not only to communicate well and be likeable, but he also had that ability to relate to people very directly and in a personal way.

I certainly can see Tim running for the Senate and winning the Senate seat in New York or even running for governor of New York and winning the governorship of New York. I don't know whether or not running for President would have been in his purview. He liked the more local-level politics than he did the federal level politics. He was more of an "I like things I can do directly" guy.

Could he have been elected president? He could do it—sure. I thought about this a long time ago. Tim would make a great New York senator. He'd make a great New York governor. He would have been a great candidate.

"He would have been a great candidate."

Tim's traits are a special gift. You can't *be* something. You have to really be it—it had to happen. Tim never had to work at it. It was a gift. Unique people like Tim Russert only come along once in a lifetime. They're special, and Tim was one of those special people without even trying. He was huge. He got the biggest funeral coverage in Washington since Ronald Reagan died in 2004. Tim had a lot of connections—people just felt connected to him. It goes back to that "gift." You can't work at it...it happens.

If, a week before he'd died, somebody had come to you and asked, "What kind of funeral do you think Tim Russert would have? Or, how big a coverage would you have to give it?" People would probably say, "Well, like another Peter Jennings." Not even close!

But it almost seemed natural. Everybody was shocked by his death. Real people "out there" really did feel connected to him.

DEEP THOUGHTS, CHEAP SHOTS AND BON MOTS

My dealings with Tim Russert were principally when he was a spokesman for Mario Cuomo, who was a new governor in 1983 and '84. Tim played an important role for Cuomo in helping him get the position of keynote speaker at the Democratic convention in 1984 in San Francisco. The description of that speech Cuomo gave was "it electrified the convention." Tim was very quick to take credit for having arranged that for the governor; whether he actually did that or not was always the subject of some discussion.

Tim was a very dynamic guy and was somebody who was very good for a reporter to deal with because he liked reporters and he tried to be helpful in a substantive way. He also liked ideas.

My impression of Tim was that he was a combination of great talent, great intelligence and great self-promotion. He was very much taken with himself and was clearly pleased to be in the lofty position of being the communications director for Mario Cuomo. That said, one also should cut him some slack because it was clear he was a very hard working, very able, broad-thinking advocate for his boss. Both Mario Cuomo and his son, Andrew Cuomo, and others around the Cuomos always had a smile on their faces when they talked about Tim. They recognized his great ability but they also had a sense of him as being on the road to *somewhere else*...that he was using his accomplishments for Mario Cuomo as a stepping stone in his own career.

In politics, there are loads of people on their way up, and Tim was one of those guys who was on his way up, trying to go somewhere else—to get to a higher position.

I was stunned when I heard that Tim was going to NBC. To me, it was anathema, especially back then, that someone who had been a political operative should be a journalist. It's become much more acceptable, but back then it was very unusual.

Tim would hang around occasionally with reporters here. He was even known to go out occasionally to a local gin mill, including one that was called Downtown Johnny's. I went out with Tim many times. When we were out with him he was, of course, very sociable and he would tell some terrific stories about his time working for Daniel Patrick Moynihan. The highlight of the story would inevitably be when he would do his impersonations of Moynihan. He was an absolute dead ringer for the very peculiar, unique accent of Moynihan which was sort of a combination of an Irish brogue, Harvard pretension and the West Side of Manhattan, where he grew up.

Tim led us to believe, without quite saying it, especially after he had three or four beers, that the West Side of Manhattan was Hell's Kitchen. His impersonation was so good that, at times, when Moynihan—who was known to take a drink or two himself, especially in the morning—there would be times when Moynihan would be so unfit to answer the phone to speak to people on the phone that he, Tim, would fill in, using this fantastic impersonation. He would always dance around the question of whether he actually had done that, but he certainly left us with the clear impression that, indeed he had, and on more than one occasion.

—**FRED DICKER**, *New York Post*, Albany bureau chief

I knew Tim Russert since 1982. When I first met Tim, I was a reporter for the *New York Daily News*, and Tim was the director of communications for Mario Cuomo when he was elected governor. I knew him from that, and obviously we both have moved on to other professions—namely television.

I've been a journalist all my life. I have never encountered anybody who was as smart or who played political chess as well as Tim Russert. When you talked to Tim, you could tell that he was thinking about things twelve moves ahead. He was extremely smart. He could play the hand out. He was an amazing man.

When I was the Albany bureau chief of the *Daily News* and he was in Albany, Tim and I saw each other on an everyday basis. I would talk with him seven days a week. After Albany, we both went off on our various whatever; we would see each other or talk to each other on various matters...and laugh. While working for Mario Cuomo, Tim made national connections as well because he was helping to push Mario Cuomo to run for president. Tim was the kind of person who maintained his friends and political connections wherever he was. Just because he wasn't working for Moynihan didn't mean he didn't talk to me and other friends all over the country, not just in Washington, on a regular basis.

With Tim it was always, "Go Bills." He was always a big sports fan...but he was also a big fan of the sport of politics. He loved politics. He ate and breathed politics. He loved sports, too, but I think, to him, politics was a sport...and it was a contact sport! Politics was the same as football to Tim. He played the game of politics as hard as anybody would play the game of football. Tim was intellectually stimulated by politics. He was a brilliant man. He was fascinated by politics and what politicians could do to change people's lives. But when he was involved in the game of politics, for Moynihan and for Cuomo—literally, it was a contact sport. It was a "take no prisoners" kind of sport for him. He was one hundred percent for the person he was working for.

Also, he was extremely adept at plotting moves. Tim is the one who was responsible for Mario Cuomo giving the keynote speech at the 1984 Democratic presidential convention and being talked about as the presidential candidate. When he went into television, I think he regarded his job on *Meet the Press* the same way. He would prepare meticulously for his programs. He would pore over what people said and how they said it. He would use their quotes to confront them because, again, it was a contact sport.

A lot of other people in the media are like that, but Tim was so much better at it. Tim was very special, very smart. Politics is something Tim was brilliant at.

At a very young age, Tim had major positions with major politicians, and he went from there to become the Washington bureau chief for NBC and from there, to go on-camera as the host of *Meet the Press*. He turned that program into *must-see* TV on Sunday mornings. It had the most impact on the political arena of any columnist or show in America.

Obviously, if you are the host of a television show, you are trying to get the politicians on, but I think that, for politicians in America, they had no choice but to be on Tim Russert's show because he was such a force on the American political scene that if you didn't "do" Tim Russert, you didn't have any validity.

—MARCIA KRAMER, writer, *New York Times*

Chapter 5

Russertpalooza

Too Much Ain't Enough

REMINISCING ABOUT THE GOOD OLD DAY

Chris Allison

Chris Allison from Pittsburgh real-ized a political junkie's dream when one of Tim Russert's classmates, Jack Bertges, arranged for a special trip to Washington, D.C. for Allison and his friend.

Even though it was almost eight years ago, I remember the day that I met Tim Russert like it was yesterday.

My friend Jack Bertges had finagled two tickets to the 2000 inauguration of President George W. Bush from his brother-in-law, John Nolen, Bob Schieffer's producer at CBS. He asked me if I would like to travel to Washington to watch history being made. Knowing that we were both very political, we got hall passes from our wives for the trip.

You remember 2000. There was a bit of a controversy regarding the election. Remember Tim Russert on NBC with his famous mini-white board? And it was a historic moment. The man who lost the popular vote but won the electoral vote was going to become our next President.

The bonus was the fact that my friend Jack went to college with Russert at John Carroll University in Cleveland.

"Let me see if I can get some tickets to see *Meet the Press*," Jack offered.

We froze our buns as we watched the inauguration, on Monday we endured below 32-degree temperatures and plenty of sleet and ice. We escaped the cold after the ceremony when Jack's brother-in-law gave us an "insider's" tour of the Capital.

We saw the cramped CBS offices in the Capitol where our tour guide worked. He and Mr. Schieffer shared a space, which could generously be described as a closet with a countertop. We also met ABC's Cokie Roberts and some other reporters.

We went into the Senate chamber and watched as new Cabinet members were confirmed. I saw Sen. Rick Santorum loitering as new officials were made official.

Here comes the part where the next morning got rough. After our tour, we went out to dinner with some of Jack's friends. One friend was a man named John Marcus, who is a pretty well-known Republican political operative. He told me that I should run for Congress. That is, if I could put together $3 million from two hundred of my closest friends.

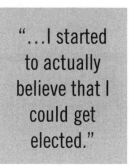

"...I started to actually believe that I could get elected."

We crashed some inauguration parties and I had way too many beers. After the fifth beer, I started to actually believe that I could get elected.

On Sunday, I was forced to roll out of bed way too early so we could get to the *Meet the Press* taping there before eight o'clock. I didn't know that *Meet the Press* wasn't live when it's broadcast at ten-thirty a.m.

Of course, we "bumped" into Karl Rove on the way in. Before that day, I didn't know who "the Architect" was back then. "Turd Blossom", as President George W. Bush calls him when he's mad, was hitting all of the Sunday morning talk shows and taped his interview even earlier.

They ushered us onto the set. My friend Jack told me to be low-key. He was a little worried that we might disturb Russert prior to taping. In bounds this bear of a guy with a big smile and bellows, "MISTER Bertges!"

Turns out, he remembered Jack, all right.

Then Senator John McCain walks in and waves. Following him were the political yin-and-yang couple, James Carville, Bill Clinton's chief strategist, and his wife Mary Matalin, one of the first President Bush's top political advisors. Go figure, huh?

Sen. McCain smiled warmly and called us "folks" as he left.

> "Russert transformed political reporting... But that's not why I'll never forget him."

The political super duo couldn't have been bothered. I was not then, nor am I now important enough for them to have much interest.

When the taping got going, I was in awe as I watched Russert, in what seemed an effortless manner, conduct the show. He listened intently and asked pointed questions in an often jovial manner. What I couldn't get over was the fact that he didn't take off his ankle-covering shoe rubbers. I marveled at the fact that the most powerful newsman in Washington was still a regular guy from Buffalo.

After the taping, I asked Mr. Russert if I could get a photo taken with him. He looked at me and smiled, saying, "Only if we can do it on the *Meet the Press* set!"

I thought then as I think today after his untimely passing—about the same age as my Dad, also as a result of a heart attack—what a helluva nice guy he was.

Here was a man who could single-handedly end a presidential candidacy while being warm and friendly to someone he never met and would never meet again. He acted like the guy at the beer distributor who offers to put your 24-pack in the trunk of your car.

Tim Russert transformed political reporting in this country. But that's not why I'll never forget him.

Even though he was a devout Irish Catholic, Tim Russert was a real mensch.

IRONICALLY ENOUGH, IT WAS SNOWING THE LAST TIME I WAS IN BUFFALO

Mark Schreiner

Schreiner went into community newspaper journalism after he left John Carroll University. He was a small-town political reporter for fifteen years. He now works in the communications office at the medical school at Duke University.

T
he summer of 1992, I was working at the John Carroll reunion. I fixed it so that I could pick Tim Russert up at the Cleveland airport. We had a great ride back to campus, and I heard a lot of his great stories.

I wanted to meet Tim very badly because we have a lot in common. We're both from the Buffalo area and our fathers were common public employees. The way it worked is that I was making a little extra money schlepping luggage at this reunion. The way they had it set up is that these university vans went back and forth to the airport with drivers to pick up alumni.

Each van had a student along to carry the bags. The buzz among my group of students had been that Russert was expected. Tim was in the class of '72, so '92 was the 20th year for that class. I got stuck on the baggage detail at the turn-around there in the parking lot. I made a friendly wager with a friend of mine that maybe if I looked on the list of names of alumni who needed pickup at the airport, I could tell if Russert was coming in. Now, this is a network guy...he'd arranged his own transportation! Well, there was his name on the list to get picked up with everybody else. I volunteered to do it. I drove across town, and Tim was there with his wife, Maureen. We rode back across town. The airport in Cleveland is on the opposite side of town from campus so it's a forty-five minute drive.

One of my questions was what had happened to him after he graduated from John Carroll. He said that after he graduated from John Carroll, he drove a taxi, that he threw bundles off the back of a newspaper distribution truck, that he was a substitute teacher. He told the story about how he was standing in line in Buffalo to be chosen to substitute teach. In Buffalo, people who wanted to substitute teach had to get up early and go down to city hall and stand in a line to see if they were needed and just wait for their assignment.

> "...that was the beginning of Tim's political career...."

Tim said he was standing in line waiting, and an old buddy of his saw him and said, "What are you doing standing in line? I can get you a job up in the mayor's office. Come work for me." So, Tim got out of line and went into the city bureaucracy...that was the beginning of Tim's political career....

I was a little kid at the time, but the signal event in the history of Buffalo, was the blizzard of 1977. I was six years old. I remember it as a huge blizzard. It brought the whole metropolitan area to a halt. We all slept in the front room of our house because both the gas and the electricity were off. We lived down in the Hamburg, New York suburban area. My father worked for the city and it took him a day or two to get home because the roads were impassable.

Russert said that Jimmy Carter had refused to declare Buffalo a disaster area, so Senator Moynihan and Senator Javits flew to Buffalo. Russert is the person who arranged it so he would pick them up at the airport and was to be their driver to tour throughout the town.

Russert said the two senators were so impressed at the level of devastation that they resolved that they were going to get right back on that plane and were going to write a joint resolution of Congress to get the emergency aid to Buffalo. Russert went right up on the plane and flew to Washington with them. That's how he got to Capitol Hill. The lesson from him to me was, "You're another common kid from Buffalo. Remember that the credentials are important, but it's also taking advantage of the opportunities that come along. You are going to need to do that." That was his message to me.

Tim had been the Buffalo guy from one of Moynihan's early campaigns, but after the blizzard of '77 was when Tim went to work for him. Tim literally left town on a plane with Moynihan...and essentially never came back. Tim worked for Moynihan for a number of years and helped him get re-elected and then he went to work for Cuomo. After he left Cuomo, he ended up at NBC.

A friend of Tim's, Pat, was a representative of the New York State Tavern Keepers Association when Tim was working for Cuomo. Pat said he and Tim helped negotiate the 21-year-old drinking age in New York. He told how there was a John Carroll connection. He said that Tim Russert had an area where he had his own entrance and exit from the governor's office, which shows how he ranked.

> "...credentials are important, but it's also taking advantage of the opportunities that come along."

QUICK HITS AND INTERESTING BITS

Around Christmas time, one of the lobbyists brought around some baskets of Hershey's candy kisses. These baskets were tied to helium balloons. Russert's at his desk, and he's pecking away at the typewriter or dictating or on the phone. He's eating those Hershey's Kisses until they are all gone...so there's no weight left in the basket. The helium balloon takes the empty basket up to the ceiling, which is like a fifteen-foot ceiling there at the Capitol Building. There's this big red helium balloon sticking to the ceiling. It stayed there for about a week until Andrew Cuomo couldn't stand it any more. He came in with a BB-pistol...and he shot the d--- thing off the ceiling....

Tim gave me some advice. Fred Dicker had a Monday column in *The New York Post*. The way it worked for people who lived downstate was that we would be picked up on Monday morning to go up on a helicopter to Albany. Russert told me, "If you are going to be picked up by the helicopter on Monday morning and, by any chance, you're reading Dicker's column as you're walking toward the helicopter, stop. Don't go any further because you could get hit by the rear rotor blade." He meant that Dicker on Monday morning could be writing something that would give a press secretary a fit. So, watch where you're going if you're reading Dicker in the *Post*—you could walk right into the rear rotor blade.

—MARTIN J. STEADMAN, former assistant to Governor Mario Cuomo

We had great intramural football teams in college. Russert wasn't the most athletic...but he was determined. We played eight-man football, and he was one of the three tackles. He was tenacious. He was determined. With him, it was just determination. What he lacked in natural ability, he made up for in determination. He wouldn't let himself be denied. He was terrific.

We had back-to-back flag football championships. It was terrific, and he was the heart and soul of that defense. I was one of the safeties. It made my job a lot easier because those guys kept rushing the quarterback. You passed on almost every down.

Russert played softball—not bad. Wasn't much of a basketball player—couldn't run a lick.

I always thought Russert might be a congressman. He really did think about running against Kemp. He was heavily involved in Erie County and Buffalo area politics. I don't know whether or not he could have beaten Kemp. He was only in his late twenties at the time. He may have been looking to come back and run in '80. Kemp, was by no means, unbeatable. Kemp won it on name recognition and because of his popularity because it was not a Republican district. From a registration standpoint, it might even have been marginally a Democratic district that Kemp "stole" with his name and popularity. I don't know how close a look Russert actually took at it. I know he talked about it and ruminated about it a little bit.

—BILL BROWN, 60, JCU '70, Atlanta

When Tim got out of law school, I was an assemblyman, and he came to me and asked if I could find employment for him since he would have to wait six or seven months for the results of the bar exam. Without any further ado, I said, "Sure," 'cause I knew Tim and his family.

In May of '76, Tim had just come with me. We had ten hearings on railroads across the state from Jamestown to Buffalo to Rochester, Syracuse, Albany. People who testified were people who had businesses on those branch lines. Tim was with me all the way. It took about two weeks to complete these hearings, driving from place to place in my car. I really got to know Tim then.

Once, we had a hearing from between Albany and Montreal. The BOT helped us out to get two extra cars on a train called the Adirondack which runs from New York City to Montreal. I wanted the two cars put on at Albany. One of those cars—I always called it the Harry Truman car—it had the porch on the back.

Every hour or so, Tim would go on that back porch and he'd yell, "Give 'em hell, Harry." He just loved Harry Truman. He was one of Tim's favorite American historical figures. I got the biggest charge out of watching him do that.

People say to me, "Tim started with you. You started him on his rise." Well, I didn't have much to do with starting him...he was so bright, and he knew where he wanted to go. It wasn't going with NBC...he was going to practice law.

After he was at NBC, I would see him once in a while. I used to represent his home town—that's how he and I came together—what we called West Seneca, New York. I was in the assembly, so I'd be marching in the Fourth of July parades. Tim was always there with his sisters, sitting on the lawn, watching the parade go by. I'd always break from the parade and go over and shake hands with him and quickly visit with him.

Tim continued to work in my office locally. The legislature was out of session. He used to tell me stories about the Moynihan campaign and was very critical of it. He'd say, "These people on this campaign are not professional enough. They don't seem to know what's going on. I don't think Moynihan will win if they don't get on the ball." He told me that four or five times.

Even at the early age of twenty-six, Tim sensed that there wasn't enough political brainpower in the Moynihan campaign... but Moynihan won very easily in 1976. Tim left me January 1, 1977 to work for Moynihan and was with him for about six years.

The first thing was, Timmy told me Moynihan had offered him a job to run the office of the Senator in Buffalo. The fellow who was supposed to be the second assistant to the senator in Washington suddenly quit...even before Moynihan was a senator. So Moynihan called Tim and said, "Never mind Buffalo...I want you to come to Washington." That's how Tim Russert got to Washington.

We'd be in the car and I'd ask Tim, "What do you think you'll be able to do with your life? "Well, I'll probably join some law firm in Buffalo. I'd like to be a trial lawyer, or even teach law." At that time, I thought to myself, "He'll find his way because he was very bright." Then, all of a sudden, he was gone. Tim was still with me when he was notified that he'd passed the bar—I think in

October. He was working with the Moynihan campaign still, so he said, "I'll just let this run until we see what comes of the Moynihan thing." Moynihan won...Tim finished out the year with me and was making plans to set up the office in Buffalo, which never happened.

Tim was with Moynihan for quite a few years. I talked to him a couple of times a month. Then, Governor Cuomo talked Tim into coming home here to New York as his press secretary. We were all surprised because Tim was chief of staff in Moynihan's office. The word in Albany was that Cuomo stole Tim from Moynihan. Russert really impressed Cuomo, and Tim was ready to move on, plus it got him back to New York.

So, then, Tim was here in Albany, and I was here in Albany. I was the sponsor in the Assembly of the death-penalty law, which never became law. I was the guy who got eighteen vetoes on that bill. I'd take a shot at the governor every once in a while. The governor wanted to raise the drinking age from nineteen to twenty-one. I led the debate on the floor, and I beat him. Then, out of that debate came a thing called the seat-belt law. I was sponsor of the seat-belt law. We were the first place in the United States with this law. Tim was with the governor at that time, and he used to call me and he would say, "You're in deep ---- now. The governor will never sign a bill with your name on it—ever!" I said, "Oh, Tim, come on.," and he'd say, "Well, I'll try to soften him up."

Tim was such a sharp guy. At the time, the governor had his eye on the Supreme Court or running for President. The Supreme Court thing was on his mind, and he wanted to do that. We had a Democratic president at the time, so he had a shot. Tim's effort to have him be the keynote speaker was along those lines. Cuomo's mother always used to say to him, "When are you going to become a judge?"

Tim's death just completely killed me. He was such a good guy.

—<u>VINCENT GRABER</u>, 74, retired New York State assemblyman

Tim's relationship with Jules Belkin? Tim was a genius. He orchestrated a deal for Belkin. He would guarantee a number—I don't know what it was, whatever the capacity was at John Carroll's gym, say it's 2,500-3,000—to Jules Belkin for any group he would bring in. What would happen is these groups would have off-days—a day with nothing booked between engagements—so Belkin would call T.J. and say, "Do you have the gym for October 8? You can have Sly and the Family Stone." Tim would say, "Yeah, let's do this." Well, Sly had a reputation for being late...not showing up. Tim told Sly and the Family Stone people that the concert was at seven-thirty. When we sold it to John Carroll, we told them the concert would start at ten o'clock at night. That's almost exactly what happened. We had our own guys go out to the airport and get Sly in a limousine to get across Cleveland to John Carroll. That guaranteed his arrival. According to the people who went out in the limousine to pick him up, it was a h--- of a ride. Let's put it this way...we don't know how he got up on stage. He showed up roughly at ten o'clock...it was a great concert....

Tim had tons of energy. I remember him in what we used to call the "Priest" car. He had a white, sterile Ford that he bought used. He drove it around his junior and senior years. I don't think he ever had enough money for gas, so I don't know how he did it. He was pretty secretive about all that stuff...people were friends, but not real close.

Tim loved nicknames. He'd see someone and would scream out their nickname! Mine was Pacells. There was Pickles Peters, Brother Love Shuba, etc. I put myself down as one of Tim's few Republican friends.

After Tim passed, the girl down the block from me was a graduate of John Carroll '87. She gets a letter from her sister. The sister knew that I was close to Tim. The sister is a nurse at the Georgetown University hospital. She writes me a note to say, "I'm sorry. I've got to tell you that I would be working the Saturday night shift, and Tim would show up for six o'clock Mass at the hospital, and if there were kids there, he would light up like a Christmas tree. He'd be talking to them, wishing them the best, shaking hands and all that. He was a phenomenal guy, going out of his way...."

I went to see *Meet the Press* one time right in the middle of the Clinton impeachment fiasco. It was a classic Russert event. Here it is, the mid-nineties, and he has two Republican congressmen and two Democratic congressmen, one for impeachment and the other against, from each side.

After the show, I got to talk to Tim. Tim always had the classic line whenever I sent a friend there: "You tell Pacelli he still owes me fifty bucks!" Any time one of my friends approached him, he'd say that. Later on, it grew to a hundred bucks.

I would be told, "Tim's gonna be at Shuba's on Saturday in Chicago." I would have my list of Republican agenda things. I'd go over point-by-point. I knew I had him. He couldn't possibly refute me. The last time I saw him, I was pent up about something and I was really ready to talk to him. "Hey, Pacelli, what's going on?" Before I even said anything about "T.J. you ignorant slut," he would say, "Oh, J.P.'s at Yale now." He knew my son, J. P., was at Yale. My son was a freshman at Tulane and we took him down there for his first day of school in New Orleans, which was twenty-four hours before Katrina hit. We left New Orleans that Sunday morning and Katrina hit that Sunday night/Monday morning, so he had to reapply to schools again. He got into Yale. But how did Tim know? He disarmed me! I forgot about my agenda.

I had something I was going to show Tim for his birthday. I was going through an old finance book from John Carroll. Flipping through it, I have a card that Tim made. It said, "Elect Russert as Student Union President, '71, the Year of the Student," and it has his picture on it. In his handwriting, it says, "Use for bookmarker."

—MARK PACELLI, JCU '72, Chicago Board of Trade

SOMETIMES GOD JUST HANDS YA ONE

Michael Gartner

Michael Gartner, the man responsible for putting Tim Russert on national television without Russert having any TV experience whatsoever, is doing what Tim Russert would have loved to do: He co-owns a minor league baseball team. His Triple-A Iowa Cubs are the top farm team for the Chicago Cubs. Gartner was president of NBC News from 1988-1993. Besides his baseball duties, Gartner is president of the Iowa Board of Regents.

Tim Russert didn't want to be on television. He was a senior executive—an inside guy, a go-to guy, an idea guy—when I joined NBC News as president in 1988. He had a background in politics, and a few months after I signed on, I asked him to head the NBC Washington bureau. He didn't want to leave New York and thought he was being shoved aside, but he very reluctantly agreed.

There were two major discussions—one was to go there to be the Washington bureau chief and the other one was to go on the air. They were very funny and very interesting. Tim Russert was smart. He did his homework. He was just a sponge for information. It might have been a risk to try that, but if we tried it and it didn't work, we'd just say, "Hey, Tim, it didn't work." Tim was a very good, smart guy. Certainly, we didn't know it was going to work that well right at first, but I probably saw that it was sooner than most. At that point, the show was a half-hour, and we decided to change it to an hour show.

In Washington, he quickly re-established old contacts—he had worked for Senator Daniel Patrick Moynihan, and he seemed to know half the town—and increasingly the morning news conferences at NBC were filled with his inside stories of this, his analyses of that and his predictions of this and that. He was always right.

"Tim," I said to him one day a year or so later, "the news call isn't supposed to be more interesting than the news shows. We've got to get across on the air the stuff you're telling us every morning. You should be on the air." "No way," he said.

Finally, I told him he should be—had to be—the moderator of *Meet the Press*, which wasn't doing well. "No way," he said again.

We argued. We debated. We fought. He raised objections…I shot them down. At the end, he said, "Look, I can't do it. I'm ugly." "Well," I said, with a laugh, "I can't argue that one"—he had a chubby face that looked like it was made out of Play-Doh—"but I'm not looking for a handsome guy. I'm looking for a smart one." Finally he agreed, and in 1991, he became moderator of the show.

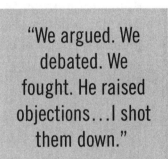

"We argued. We debated. We fought. He raised objections…I shot them down."

I had some sweatshirts made up with his picture on the front. "Tim Russert," they said. "Not just a pretty face." He was, eventually, amused.

He was made for the job. His training from his Jesuits had sharpened his mind, his lessons from his father had instilled his values, his life in politics had widened his knowledge, and his training as a lawyer had honed his questioning. The show was almost an overnight success, and soon we expanded it to a full hour. Then he—and it—took off.

Tim was a terrific moderator for *Meet the Press*. He was a good friend. He was a smart guy who always did his homework. He was fair—right down the middle. When he first went on, everyone said, "Oh, you can't do this or that. He's a liberal who worked for Cuomo and Moynihan." After he was on, we'd get as many complaints from liberal viewers as we would from conservatives—about fifty-

fifty. Both would say he was unfair—he was one-sided. That was bulls---! He did his homework, and he evolved. He wasn't spectacular from the first day, but he evolved. The show got better and better. Tim got better and better. Pretty soon, nobody was on there but him. When he first started, there was a moderator, panelists and a guest. There were fewer panelists and fewer panelists... finally it was just Tim and a guest. And that worked out great.

He used old-fashioned tools in a new-fashioned industry. He used a chalkboard like a coach. He put words—words, of all things!—on the screen to make his point. He was as tough as he was fair, as demanding of himself as he was of his guests. He prepared for each show as if it were a final exam.

> "He used old-fashioned tools in a new-fashioned industry."

Most of all, he was believable. That face turned out to be what my father called "an affidavit face." You looked at him and you just knew he was telling you the truth.

The show made him rich and famous. I don't know how rich, but a few years ago when he signed a new, long-term contract with NBC, he called me up to tell me, and he remembered his reluctance about taking the job. He laughed, and he said, "I thank you. My wife thanks you. My son thanks you...and my unborn grandchildren, however many there will be, thank you." It must have been a good deal.

But no matter how rich and famous he became, he always came across on television as a nice guy—who couldn't like a guy who loved Buffalo and who wished his dad Happy Father's Day on the air?—but he was more than nice. He was kind...he was caring... and he was generous.

My kids loved him. All kids loved him. My kids would come to New York to visit me early on, and Russert had the office right next to mine before he went to Washington. He'd always come in and my kids would be so happy to see him. He treated them as adults, and he listened to them.

A few years ago, I called him and asked if he'd make a big speech in Des Moines, where I live. It was part of a lecture series at Drake University. I knew he was in great demand, I said, but I asked if he'd do it as a favor for me. "They'll pay you $30,000," I added. He didn't think twice. "I'll do it under one condition," he said, "The $30,000 goes to that program for kids that is Christopher's memorial."

> "And...that was the deal... and Tim was exactly right."

My 17-year-old son, Christopher, died in 1994. He was hit by a severe initial attack of juvenile diabetes, right out of the blue. I'd left NBC by then and was back here in Des Moines. When my friends at NBC heard about it, they passed the word around. Russert called me right away. He was in tears...I was in tears. Russert said, "Think of it this way. If God had come to you seventeen years ago and said to you, 'I'll give you a healthy, happy, terrific kid named Christopher for seventeen years, and that's it,' you'd have made the deal." And...that was the deal...and Tim was exactly right. Luke, at his dad's funeral services, related that story and remembered it, "If God offered me a Dad that great but I could only have him for 22 years..."

I wrote that in a piece about Christopher two days after Christopher died. At the time, I was a columnist for *USA Today*. I ended the article with Tim's quote. Both Russert and I got inundated with e-mails and letters and calls about it. As it happened, that would have been the first week in July of 1994. Later that fall at the Al Smith dinner, a political dinner in New York, Tim was sitting next to whomever the Cardinal was at the time. Tim was telling the Cardinal about Christopher and about the column I wrote and about the reaction. The Cardinal said, "Tell me more." But, Tim said that just then the dinner started, so they couldn't continue the conversation. Later, Tim wrote him about it, and the Cardinal at St.

Patrick's Cathedral on All Saints' Day or All Fools' Day or whatever that is that the Catholic Church has on November 1, gave a sermon all about Russert and Christopher. I didn't know anything about it except somebody sent me a printed copy of the sermon.

> "As it turns out, there was a similar deal— the terms were 58 years— with Tim."

Tim was right, of course that was the deal— I just didn't know it.

As it turns out, there was a similar deal— the terms were fifty-eight years—with Tim.

We just didn't know it. But we—his family, his friends, his guests and his viewers, all of us so enriched by him—would have made it in a second.

GO BILLS!

Other Books by Rich Wolfe

Da Coach (Mike Ditka)
I Remember Harry Caray
There's No Expiration Date on Dreams (Tom Brady)
He Graduated Life with Honors and No Regrets (Pat Tillman)
Take This Job and Love It (Jon Gruden)
Been There, Shoulda Done That (John Daly)
Oh, What a Knight (Bob Knight)
And the Last Shall Be First (Kurt Warner)
Remembering Jack Buck
Sports Fans Who Made Headlines
Fandemonium
Remembering Dale Earnhardt
For Yankees Fans Only
For Cubs Fans Only
For Red Sox Fans Only
For Cardinals Fans Only
For Packers Fans Only
For Hawkeyes Fans Only
For Browns Fans Only
For Mets Fans Only
For Notre Dame Fans Only—The New Saturday Bible
For Bronco Fans Only
For Nebraska Fans Only
For Buckeye Fans Only
For Georgia Bulldog Fans Only
For South Carolina Fans Only
For Clemson Fans Only
For Cubs Fans Only—Volume II
For Oklahoma Fans Only
For Yankees Fans Only—Volume II

Questions? Contact the author directly at 602-738-5889.

"...IT ALL COMES DOWN TO THIS..."